Butter In The Bard

Also by

Robert Bernoskie

A trio of board games:

**Food Lovers Food Trivia
Dieters Roulette
Clean Your Plate**

———————

1991 Author of:

**Food For Thought,
Tasteful Trivia For Beginning
And
Seasoned Food Lovers**

———————

Forthcoming:

Cooking With Shakespeare

See page 168 for details

Butter In The Bard

Reading Between The Viands

Of

Wᴹ. Shakespeare

Robert D. Bernoskie

Original Traveling Chef
Rosemead, California

Printed in the United States of America

Original Traveling Chef considers for publication original works
in the culinary, literary
and humanitarian areas.
Send inquiries to the above address.

———————————

ISBN: 0-9628283-1-9

LIBRARY OF CONGRESS CATALOG CARD NUMBER: 91-90346

Shakespeare, William 1564-1616.
    Butter in the bard : reading between the viands of Wm.
Shakespeare / Robert D. Bernoskie.
    p. cm.
    Includes bibliographical references and index.

    1. Cookery. 2. Food. I. Bernoskie, Robert D. II. Title.
TX645   641.5
                                          QB191-1315

To Our Youth

*The connoisseurs, food lovers,
and humanitarians of the future.
And especially to the young
people of Don Bosco Tech, who have
been these past ten years, the
seasoning in my life.*

About the Cover

William Shakespeare (Gregory Bell) amid a serendipitous array of now-celebrated Shakespearean viands (articles of food), that have given birth to the new culinary genre, *Chefspearean Cooking.* "A lemon suck with cloves," (Love's Labour's Lost, Act 5, Scene 2) mirrors the features of Comedy and Tragedy, while in the background, a white chocolate bust of The Bard, is encircled by the poetic spices of marjorom, rosemary and thyme.

* * *

Having appeared in over sixty plays, actor/writer/director Gregory Bell (William Shakespeare), has gained international repute as the living representation of The Bard. With a countenance that has been captured for **People Magazine** and in hologram form for a U.K. Cheque Guarantee Card called *The Bard Card*, Mr. Bell has performed benefits for *The Shakespeare Globe Centre of London; The Shakespeare Round Table; The Los Angeles Master Chorale; Serra A.I.D.S. Project; Past Times With Good Companie,* (U.S. and England); *Daybreak for Women;* and, *Bridal Faire '90.* Mr. Bell is currently performing in his one-man play, *Alms for Oblivion, An Evening with Will.*

Cover Design and Concept: Original Traveling Chef
Photography: John Aydelotte Studios
Interior Illustrations: Conceptualine
A special thanks to Sharon Silvia

Table Of Contents

| Sir Toby: | *Does not our life consist of the four elements?* |
| Sir Andrew: | *Faith, so they say, but I think it rather consists of eating and drinking.* |

Twelfth Night, 2,3

The Truth About Shakespeare

To eat or not to eat? That was the question, served to me on firm tones by my good and watchful physician after my annual physical.

"But doctor..." I pleaded, while negotiating an expanding waist into yesteryear trousers.

"There are no buts!" was the hastened reply.

"The sauces, sweets, in-betweeners, Polish wieners, third helpings, little samplings and all wines are out!," he repeated.

"Then I'll home with me and straight to bed," I grunted, "To sleep, perchance to dine, — er dream."

"Get off it Bob, you can do it," was the gruff reassurance. "And in forty-five pounds from now you'll be thanking me for the advice."

(With all things considered, the doctor's diagnosis was undisputed. Alas, poor Yorkshire! Given my six foot height, medium frame and impassioned love for food, I was overweight at 205 pounds and at age thirty-three the moment was ripe to reverse the trend.)

"It's time for you to start winning at losing," the doctor prompted. "To enter your winter of discontent, content in the hope that your appetite will no longer be as deep as a well nor as wide as a church door," he chuckled.

"Doctor," I sparked, making my way to the outer office, "I'll try it. But believe me, the lure of food wields a mighty spatula over me."

"What you need to do, mister vast roundure of a chef, is reactivate some non-food related interests to cushion those peak moments of dietetic weakness. A little reading perhaps? Say, Si-Fi?"
"No." I replied.
"Thrillers?"
"No."
"History?"
"No."
"Bio's?"
"No."
"Literary works then? Say, Shakespeare?"
"Huh?"
"Shakespeare. The poems... the plays... you know."

The doctor was an avid Shakespearean who could quote from practiced memory an impressive number of verses. For myself, the suggestion didn't exactly move me into finger spinning some pizza dough, but neither did it disinterest me.

"With an Achilles heel in my stomach, doc, I might as well try something," I said, shaking his hand good-bye. "I'll be back for that follow-up in a few months."

I picked up the telephone. It was my doctor's secretary confirming yet another appointment in one week and reminding me of the physician's advice that "A William a day keeps the food at bay." I politely hung up.

Meals, from my perspective, had become one bleak enterprise after another. For the past ten months I had learned the definition of spartan, and in efforts to circumvent cooking and eating frenzies, I digested my own helpings from the likes of Browning, Aristotle and Michner.

"The doctor will radiate at the loss of near forty pounds," I considered. "But this lean living can't go on much longer." I also knew it was time to crack open another volume of something, but what?

Earlier in the day I had covetously browsed at one of those fancy food bazaars, and the urge to indulge was becoming unrelenting as evening approached. "All right," I surrendered, making my way to the bookshelf. "The doctor's remedy — the Shakespeare! The plays!" The big guns I was ever confident in retreating behind when snack attacks became BLINTZKRIEGS. Seating myself at the kitchen table (for better lighting, of course) I opened to the complete plays of The Bard and began to scan...

"William Shakespeare...baptized April 26, 1564...Globe Theatre...First Folio...etc." I turned to the contents. To placate the doctor, I ventured to choose a work paralleling my present dietetic condition. A comedy? A tragedy? An historical play?... A porterhouse with mashed potatoes and gra...

I urged myself to resist, and to settle into something divertingly safe and rich with quick and able insight into the human condition then and now. In other words, follow the doctor's orders. Adjusting the area lamp and facing away from the refrigerator, I began with *The Tragedy of King Lear*.

"Deep stuff," I thought, "the ingratitude of offspring."

"Poor old king."

"You tell 'em."

(a stomach growl)

"*King Lear: Five days we do allot thee, for provision*
To shield thee from diseases of the world;
And, on the sixth, to turn thy hated back
Upon our kingdom: if, on the tenth day following,
Thy banish'd trunk be found in our dominions,
The moment is thy death. Away! By Jupiter,
This shall not be revok'd!"

"This is powerful."

(another stomach growl)

"King Lear: Thou hast her, France: let her be
thine: for we
Have no such daughter, nor shall ever see
That face of hers again: — therefore be gone,
Without our grace, our love, our benison."

"How intense," I considered.

"Hold my course. Prepare for dinner."

"Say What?!"

"Hold my course. Prepare for dinner."

"Thou shalt serve me."

"Pay no attention Robert," I unsteadily cautioned.

"Dinner, ho, dinner."

Quickly I paged to another and then another play, ...but
only to be equally dumbfounded.

"Eat. I pray you."

"And this is doctor's advice?" I trembled.

"...Will you have some more sauce?"

"This piece of toasted cheese."

"This salivating mouth," I intoned. "Come on, hold the bacon, please!"

"Hang hog is latin for BACON, I warrant you."

"O dear God," I prayed.

"A glass of Madeira and a cold capon's leg."

"I'mmmmmm going to lose it!"

"Those kissing cherries tempting grow."

I held my ground until vicarious participation shamelessly placed me in the character of Orlando (As You Like It, 2,7) whose immediate feelings irreversibly intensified my own:

> *"I almost die for food and let me have it."*
> *"Let me have it!"* I repeated loud and longing.
> *"Let me have it!!!"*
> *"Let Me..."*

The kitchen was never so easy and guiltless a conquest. From that night and for days thereafter, bread and bard, 'er became a welcomed side dish to some wonderful feasting.

The doctor pointed to the scale. "Over here, please."

"HONORIFICABILITUDINITATIBUS," whizzed from his lips as he stared me in the eyes.

"Are you talkin' to me?" I asked stepping on the scale.

"HONORIFICABILITUDINITATIBUS" he repeated, with slow and formed enunciation. "It's an exaggerated form of the word honorable used in Love's Labour's Lost, Act 5, Scene 1."

"You don't say," I replied while glancing at my feet — or what I could see of them after several days of hearty dining.

"Looks t' me like somebody's been in the cookie jar," the doctor said while notating in his chart. "Up eight pounds." I stepped from the scale foolishly hoping not to be seen. The doctor came forward and, placing a fatherly arm around my shoulder, began to shake his head in dismay.

"I will be a fool in question, hoping to be the wiser by your answer. All's Well That Ends Well, Act 2, Scene 2," he quoted.

"What was the question?" I said.

"No, No, No," he lamented. "I was under the impression you were serious about this diet. You came to me concerned. We agreed. Your visits were regular, my advice sound, and your weight-loss consistent. Now however... Have you been reading?... I mean during your periods of desire?"

"Yes, but..."

"There are no buts!"

"What were you reading? Sister Carbonara of The Forty Sauces? I'm no fool you know!" he insisted.

The doctor continued, often in rather poetic tongue lashing and ended his scolding with an earnest plea to lay off the sweets and lay on the Shakespeare.

I was silent as I left his office that day. I hadn't the heart to tell him that taken collectively, the evidence I discovered was compelling: *Shakespeare,* thy name is *Chef!* and probably a good one; an *epicurean rascal* (The Merry Wives of Windsor, 2,2). Yet with the dreaded black plague, a trickle of new herbs and spices from far off regions and the fork just a play toy at the common table, how successful would any culinary professional be during that era, save to drape his viands in verse and pass them off as the finest plays the world has 'er seen. Leave it to a foodie!

His words are a
very fantastical banquet.
Benedick, Much Ado About Nothing, 2,3

Lifting The Lid After 400 Years

The works of William Shakespeare (1564-1616) contain a drumbeat for everyone. But in my case, a *drumstick,* (Bertram, All's Well That Ends Well, 3,6); and even a nod to one of our culinary heroines, *"Julietta with child."* (Mistress Overdone, Measure For Measure, 1,2)

To be sure, Shakespeare is not all that noted for *his viands sparkling in a golden cup* (III Henry VI, 2,5). According to The Harvard Concordance To Shakespeare, (Belknap Press, 1973) there are 884,647 words in the entire works of William Shakespeare. By direct, indirect and/or homographic association only a cupful of these words by comparison, convey any culinary significance... But there they are and there they'll stay. For beneath the sauces of high drama and intrigue (and having been overlooked and unappreciated for over four centuries) are in among the rest, those tasty morsels from the culinary garden, sown and cultivated by The Bard himself with no less care, I am sure, than the most eloquent of his "non-viandular" passages.

Now, after four-hundred years,
and with a touch more prominence —
the Shakespearean roster of

VIANDS IN VERSE.

The Shakespearean Viands *

a-brewing • 1 **

abstaining • 2

abstinence • 5

acre • 3

acres • 4

a-ducking • 1

a-feasting • 1

a-field • 4

afresh • 5

after-dinner's • 2

after-nourishment • 1

after-supper • 2

a-hungry • 2

a-hunting • 2

ale • 13

alehouse' • 1

alehouse • 8

alehouses • 1

ales • 2

ale-wash'd • 1

ale-wife • 1

ale-wive's • 1

all-eating • 1

alligator • 1

almond • 1

alms-drink • 1

anchoves • 1

angle • 9

angled • 1

angler • 1

angling • 4

an-hungry • 1

animal • 3

animals • 5

appetite • 43

appetites • 5

apple • 10

apple-John • 2

apple-Johns • 2

apples • 3

apple-tart • 1

apricock • 1

apricocks • 2

apron • 2

apron-men • 1

aprons • 5

aqua-vitae • 6

a-ripening • 1

aspic • 2

aspic's • 1

aspics' • 1

ate • 3

ates • 2

baa • 1

Bacchus • 2

bacon • 3

bacon-fed • 1

bacons • 1

baes • 2

bait • 19

baited • 5

baiting • 1

baiting-place • 1

* The word <u>viands</u> as used in this heading as well as the word <u>butter</u> as used in the title of this book are employed as metaphoric designations to signify a wide range of culinary activity, association and, of course, the many instances of the viand itself.

** The number following each word in this listing denotes the total number of times that word appears in the entire works of William Shakespeare acquired by direct reading and subsequent verification with <u>The Harvard Concordance to Shakespeare.</u>

baits • 4
bak'd • 6
bak'd-meats • 1
bake • 2
baked • 1
baker's • 1
bakers' • 1
bakes • 1
baking • 1
banbury • 1
banquet • 15
banqueted • 1
banqueting • 2
banquets • 2
barley • 1
barley-break • 1
barley-broth • 1
barn • 2
barrels • 1
barrow • 1
basket • 20
basted • 1
bastes • 1
basting • 2
batch • 1
bays • 2
bay-trees • 1
bean-fed • 1
beans • 1
beast-eating • 1
bee • 7
beef • 12
beefs • 2
beef-witted • 1
beehives • 1
beer • 5
beer-barrel • 1

bee's • 1
bees • 9
belch • 6
belch'd • 1
belches • 1
belching • 2
bellies • 2
belly • 38
bellyful • 2
belly-pinched • 1
belly's • 3
berries • 8
berry • 3
bespice • 1
beverage • 1
big-bellied • 1
bilberry • 1
bird • 50
bird's • 4
birds • 48
biscuit • 2
bit • 8
bite • 40
bites • 11
biting • 10
bits • 6
bitter • 76
bitterest • 2
bitterly • 9
bitterness • 11
bitt'rest • 2
blackberries • 2
blackberry • 1
blanch • 10
blanch'd • 1
bleat • 3
bleated • 1

bleats • 1
blend • 2
blended • 2
blent • 2
bloom • 2
bloom'd • 2
blooming • 1
blossom • 13
blossoming • 2
blossoms • 7
boar • 35
boar-pig • 1
boar's • 1
boar-spear • 1
boil • 7
boil'd • 4
boil'd-brains • 1
boiling • 4
bone • 18
bones • 84
bottle • 20
bottle-ale • 2
bottled • 2
bottles • 3
bough • 6
boughs • 11
bowl • 13
bowls • 3
brains • 45
bran • 7
bread • 26
bread-chipper • 1
breakfast • 16
breast • 118
breasts • 14
brew • 4
brewage • 1

brew'd • 3

brewer's • 2

brewers • 1

brew-house • 1

brewing • 1

brews • 1

brimful • 4

brine • 11

brine-pit • 1

brine-pits • 1

broil'd • 1

broils • 13

broth • 1

broths • 1

buffet • 4

buffets • 5

bullcalf • 8

bull's • 3

bulls • 4

bunch • 2

bunches • 2

Burdeaux • 8

burgher • 1

burghers • 2

burgundy • 41

burn • 89

bushel • 1

bushels • 1

butcher • 20

butcher'd • 3

butchered • 4

butcheries • 2

butcher's • 4

butchers • 7

butler • 4

butt-end • 1

butter • 8

butter'd • 2

butter-woman's • 1

butter-women's • 1

buttery • 1

butt'ring • 1

butt'ry-bar • 1

by-drinkings • 1

cabbage • 1

cackling • 2

cain-color'd • 1

cake • 4

cake's • 1

cakes • 4

calf • 17

calves • 1

calve's-head • 1

camel • 5

canaries • 2

canary • 6

candied • 3

candy • 2

cannibals • 4

caper • 6

capers • 3

capon • 8

capon's • 2

capons • 2

carbinado • 1

carbinado'd • 1

carbonado • 2

carbonado'd • 1

caret • 2

carp • 3

carv'd • 7

carve • 11

carved • 3

carver • 1

carver's • 1

carves • 1

carving • 2

cask • 1

caters • 1

cates • 4

cattle • 5

cauldron • 8

caviare • 1 (caviary)

celebration • 7

Ceres' • 3

Ceres • 4

cestern • 3

cesterns • 1

chaff • 10

charneco • 1

cheese • 13

cheese-paring • 1

cherries • 3

cherry • 9

cherry-pit • 1

cherry-stone • 1

chestnut • 3

chestnuts • 1

chew • 2

chew'd • 2

chewing • 1

chick • 1

chicken • 3

chickens • 4

chops • 4

chuck • 7

churn • 1

claret • 1

climate • 8

cloves • 1

cluck'd • 1

22

cobbler • 2
codling • 1
cod's • 1
cods • 1
cogscomb • 1
confection • 1
confectionary • 1
confections • 1
consume • 11
cook • 16
cook'd • 2
cookery • 2
cooks • 3
core • 4
cork • 2
corn • 36
corn-field • 1
cornish • 2
corn's • 1
corns • 2
course • 172
courses • 19
cow • 7
cowish • 1
coxcomb • 20
coxcombs • 4
crab • 10
crabbed • 4
crab's • 1
crabs • 2
crab-tree • 2
crab-trees • 1
crave • 51
craves • 27
craving • 5
cream • 5
cream-fac'd • 1

crisp • 3
crocadile • 1
crocodile • 4
crop • 10
cropp'd • 8
crops • 2
crow • 31
crows • 18
crumb • 1
crumble • 1
crumbs • 1
crush • 13
crust • 4
crusts • 1
crusty • 1
cup • 49
cupbearer • 2
cupboarding • 1
cups • 8
curd • 2
curds • 3
currants • 1
custard • 1
custard-coffin • 1
cut • 181
cuts • 13
cutting • 8
damsons • 1
danish • 5
date • 23
dates • 5
deer • 42
deer's • 2
delectable • 2
delicious • 4
deliciousness • 1
delights • 21

desert • 48
deserts • 21
devour • 14
devour'd • 6
devoured •2
devourers • 1
devouring • 8
devours • 4
dewberries • 1
diet • 18
dieted • 5
dieter • 1
digest • 10
digested • 5
digestion • 6
digestions • 1
digest/'t • 1
din'd • 17
dine • 25
diner • 1
dines • 2
dining-chamber • 1
dining-chambers • 1
dinner • 83
dinner's • 2
dinners • 2
dinner-time • 10
dip • 3
dips • 1
dish • 33
dish'd • 1
dishes • 9
disroot • 1
dissolv'd • 6
dissolve • 10
dissolved • 1
dissolves • 3

23

distaste • 4

distasted • 1

distasteful • 1

distill • 4

distillation • 2

distill'd • 11

distilling • 2

distillment • 1

distills • 1

doe • 9

dogberry • 1

dogfish • 1

double-henn'd • 1

dough • 2

doughy • 1

dove • 24

dove's • 2

doves' • 1

doves • 12

draught • 10

draughts • 3

drink • 164

drinking • 25

drinkings • 1

drinks • 18

drink'st • 2

drunk • 69

drunkard • 12

drunkard's • 1

drunkards • 6

drunken • 22

drunkenly • 1

drunkenness • 4

drunk'st • 1

duck • 11

ducks • 4

ears • 183

eat • 160

eaten • 19

eater • 4

eating • 14

eats • 20

eel • 5

eels • 2

eel-skin • 2

eelskins • 1

egg • 14

eggs • 8

egg-shell • 1

egg-shells • 1

eisel • 1

enrich'd • 11

epicure • 1

epicurean • 2

ewe • 4

ewer • 1

ewers • 1

ewes • 11

ew'r • 1

exercise • 20

fallow • 3

fallows • 1

famine • 12

famish • 10

famish'd • 11

famishing • 1

farm • 8

farmer • 1

farmer's • 3

farm-house • 1

farms • 1

farrow • 1

fasted • 1

fasting • 13

fasting-days • 1

fast-lost • 1

fasts • 4

fat • 71

fat-already • 1

fat-guts • 1

fatness • 1

fat's • 1

fats • 1

fatted • 2

fatter • 1

fattest • 2

fatting • 2

fawns • 2

feast • 108

feasted • 5

feast-finding • 1

feasting • 10

feast's • 1

feasts • 18

feast-won • 1

fed • 39

feed • 93

feeder • 6

feeders • 3

feedeth • 2

feeding • 17

feeds • 23

feed'st • 3

field • 167

fields • 31

fig • 6

figs • 4

fig's-end • 1

filberts • 1

fillet • 2

filling • 9

fin • 3
finch • 1
finch-egg • 1
fine-baited • 1
fins • 2
first-fruits • 1
fish • 48
fish'd • 2
fisher • 2
fishermen • 5
fishermen's • 1
fishers • 2
fishes • 13
fishfield • 1
fish-like • 1
fish-meals • 1
fishmonger • 2
fishpond • 1
flagon • 1
flap-jacks • 1
flask • 2
flock • 19
flocks • 7
florentine • 9
flour • 1
flowers • 57
flow'rs • 22
fodder • 1
food • 71
fowl • 15
fowls • 4
fragment • 3
fragments • 4
freshness • 40
froth • 16
frothy • 1
fruit • 37

fruit-dish • 1
fruiterer • 1
fruitful • 15
fruits • 9
fruit-tree • 1
fruit-trees • 2
fry • 8
frying • 1
full-fed • 1
gallons • 1
gammon • 1
garden • 35
gardener • 1
gardeners • 3
garden-house • 3
garden's • 1
gardens • 3
garlic • 4
garlic-eaters • 1
garnish • 2
garnish'd • 2
garnished • 1
geese • 11
gills • 2
gin • 4
ginger • 7
gingerbread • 1
glasses • 11
glutt'nous • 1
glutton • 5
gluttoning • 1
glutton-like • 1
glutton's • 1
gluttony • 2
goat • 7
goatish • 1
goats • 9

goblet • 2
goblets • 1
goose • 29
gooseberry • 1
goose-look • 1
gormandizing • 1
gosling • 2
gourd • 1
grain • 18
grained • 4
grains • 3
grape • 6
grapes • 9
gravy • 3
grease • 7
greases • 1
greasily • 1
greasy • 10
grove • 18
groves • 5
gruel • 1
guest • 38
guests • 18
gurmandize • 1
half-supp'd • 1
hams • 3
hang-hog • 1
hare • 19
hares • 4
harvest • 18
harvest-home • 2
harvest-man • 1
hazel-nut • 1
hazel-nuts • 1
health • 110
healthful • 10
health-giving • 1

healths • 4
healthsome • 1
healthy • 2
heart-burn'd • 1
heart-burnt • 1
hearth • 3
hearths • 1
heat • 78
heated • 6
hen • 8
hens • 1
herb • 9
herbs • 11
herb-woman • 1
herd • 18
herdmen • 1
herds • 4
herdsman • 1
herdsmen • 2
herring • 6
herrings • 2
hive • 8
hives • 1
hog • 6
hogs • 2
hogshead • 5
hogsheads • 1
honey • 38
honey-bag • 3
honey-bags • 1
honey-bees • 1
honeycomb • 1
honey-dew • 1
honey-drops • 1
honeyed • 1
honey-heavy • 1
honey-sweet • 3

honey-tongued • 1
host • 70
hostess' • 1
hostess • 30
hunger • 17
hungerly • 3
hunger's • 2
hunger-starved • 1
hungry • 25
hungry-starved • 1
hunt • 35
hunted • 7
hunter • 9
hunter's • 3
hunters' • 1
hunters • 2
hunteth • 1
hunting • 17
huntress' • 1
huntress • 1
hunts • 3
huntsman • 7
huntsmen • 4
hunt'st • 1
husks • 5
hyssop • 1
ice • 21
ill-roasted • 1
inch-meal • 1
indigested • 2
jelly • 3
joints • 21
juice • 7
julia • 27
keel • 4
kernel • 4
kernels • 2

kidney • 1
kitchen • 6
kitchen'd • 1
kitchens • 2
knead • 1
kneaded • 1
kneading • 2
knives • 12
lamb • 39
lambs • 14
larded • 4
larding • 1
lards • 3
leas • 3
leather-coats • 1
leaven • 2
leaven'd • 1
leavening • 2
leek • 13
leeks • 5
legs • 77
lemon • 1
lettuce • 1
lime • 12
liquor • 18
liquorish • 1
liquors • 2
liver • 18
livers • 10
loaf • 2
mace • 4
maces • 1
malt • 1
manna • 1
manners • 77
Manningtree ox • 1
marjerom • 1

marjorom • 1
marjorum • 1
market • 16
market-place 24
market-price • 1
meal • 11
meal'd • 1
meals • 6
mealy • 1
measure • 94
measures • 11
meat • 70
meats • 2
medlar • 6
medlars • 1
melt • 31
melting • 11
melts • 6
mess • 11
milk • 25
milk'd • 2
milking-time • 1
milk-liver'd • 1
milkmaid • 2
milks • 2
milk-white • 6
milky • 3
mince • 5
mints • 1
mounch'd • 3
mouth • 132
mouthful • 1
mulberries • 3
mulberry • 2
munch • 1
mustard • 9
mustardseed • 6

mutton • 11
muttons • 2
napkin • 14
napkins • 4
neat • 11
neat-herd's • 1
neat's • 3
nectar • 4
nibbling • 3
nose-herbs • 1
nourish • 7
nourish'd • 8
nourishing • 1
nourishment • 4
nut • 6
nutmeg • 2
nutmegs • 1
nuts • 2
nutshell • 2
oat • 1
oatcake • 1
oats • 5
o'er-eaten • 1
o'erfed • 1
o'er-leavens • 1
offal • 3
oil • 15
olive • 5
olives • 2
olive-trees • 1
onion • 2
onion-ey'd • 1
onions • 2
orange • 2
orchard • 17
orchards • 2
ort • 2

orts • 2
ounce • 6
ounces • 1
outsweet'ned • 1
oven • 3
oven's • 1
overdone • 3
over-measure • 1
over-ripen'd • 1
over-roasted • 2
ox • 11
ox-beef • 1
oxen • 7
oyster • 7
oyster-wench • 1
palate • 10
palates • 6
pancake • 1
pancakes • 3
pannier • 1
pantler • 4
pantry • 1
paring • 1
paring-knife • 1
parsley • 1
parsnip • 1
parsnips • 1
partridge • 2
paste • 5
pasture • 12
pasty • 2
peach • 1
peach-color'd • 2
peaches • 1
pear • 5
pears • 1
peas • 2

sage • 7

salad • 1

sallet • 5

sallets • 3

salmon • 1

salmon's • 1

salmons • 1

salt • 45

salt-butter • 1

salter • 1

salt-fish • 1

saltiers • 1

saltness • 1

salt-water • 2

sauce • 17

saucers • 1

sauces • 1

savor • 10

savoring • 1

savors • 8

savory • 3

scald • 8

scalded • 1

scalding • 2

scour • 8

season • 46

season'd • 8

seasoned • 1

seasoning • 1

seasons • 10

seed • 6

seeded • 2

seeds • 10

seedsman • 1

serve • 193

shanks • 3

shark • 2

sheep • 44

sheep's • 4

sheeps • 1

sherris • 4

shrimp • 2

sieve • 4

sip • 3

sipp'd • 1

sipping • 1

skillet • 1

skim-milk • 1

slaughter-house • 7

slice • 2

smack • 9

smacking • 1

smacks • 2

smell • 56

smelling • 6

smells • 15

smelt • 7

smoke • 27

snail • 8

sop • 3

sops • 2

sour • 36

sour'd • 1

sourest • 4

souring • 2

sourly • 3

sours • 2

sous'd • 1

souse • 1

sow • 9

sow'd • 5

sowing • 1

sows • 1

sparrow • 9

spice • 3

spiced • 1

spicery • 1

spices • 8

spoon-meat • 1

sprigs • 1

squash • 3

stale • 27

staleness • 1

standing-bowl • 1

starv'd • 12

starve • 17

starved • 5

steer • 4

stew • 2

steward • 22

stew'd • 9

stews • 2

stir • 87

stock • 26

stock-fish • 2

stomach • 46

stomachs • 15

store-house • 3

strawberries • 3

strawberry • 1

stuffing • 2

sugar • 15

sugar-candy • 1

sugarsop • 1

sup • 21

supp'd • 7

supper • 51

suppers • 1

supper-time • 10

supping • 1

sups • 5

swallow'd • 16	tavern • 9	viands • 8
swallowed • 7	thighs • 4	victual • 2
swallowing • 8	thyme • 2	vict'lers • 1
swan • 9	tine • 3	(victualers)
swan's • 3	toast • 3	victuall'd • 1
sweet • 876	toasted • 3	victuals • 4
sweeten • 8	toasting-iron • 1	vine • 9
sweetens • 1	toasts • 1	vinegar • 3
sweeter • 19	toasts-and-butter • 1	vines • 4
sweetest • 27	toothpick • 2	vineyard • 5
sweetly • 35	turkey • 2	vineyards • 2
sweetmeats • 2	turkeys • 1	wafer-cakes • 1
sweet'ned • 1	turnips • 1	walnut • 1
sweetness • 13	turtle • 7	walnut-shell • 1
sweets • 18	turtles • 5	warden • 1
sweet-savor'd • 1	under-skinker • 1	wassail • 3
sweet-season'd • 1	unfed • 1	water • 141
sweet-smelling • 1	unripe • 4	wheat • 8
sweet'st • 4	unseasoned • 1	whites • 1
tallow • 5	utensil • 1	wild-fowl • 2
tart • 3	utensils • 2	wild-goose • 1
tartness • 2	vapor • 10	wine • 82
taste • 95	vapors • 12	worts • 2
tasted • 9	veal • 2	wren • 7
tasteful • 1	vegetives • 1	ye(a)st • 1
tastes • 4	venison • 7	ye(a)sty • 2
tasting • 2	viand • 1	

The Final Count: 10,710

Shakespearean Favorites

dinner • 83; drink • 164; eat • 160; feast • 108; feed • 93; food • 74; health • 110; host • 70; meat • 70; mouth • 132; pluck • 115; serve • 193; smell • 56; stir • 87; stomach • 46; supper • 51; sweet • 876; taste • 95; wine • 82

The Liberation Of The Viands

The body of this book is divided into seventeen *Chefspearean Classifications* according to culinary subject. All quotations in these classifications and throughout are copied verbatim from the following (complete) plays of William Shakespeare.

THE COMEDIES

A Midsummer Night's Dream

All's Well That Ends Well

As You Like It

The Comedy Of Errors

Love's Labour's Lost

Measure For Measure

The Merchant Of Venice

The Merry Wives Of Windsor

Much Ado About Nothing

The Taming Of The Shrew

The Tempest

Twelfth Night Or What You Will

The Two Gentleman Of Verona

The Winter's Tale

THE HISTORIES

I Henry IV

II Henry IV

Henry V

I Henry VI

II Henry VI

III Henry VI

Henry VIII

King John

Richard II

Richard III

THE TRAGEDIES

Antony And Cleopatra

Coriolanus

Cymbeline

Hamlet

Julius Caesar

King Lear

Macbeth

Othello, The Moore Of Venice

Pericles, Prince Of Tyre

Romeo And Juliet

Timon Of Athens

Titus Andronicus

Troilus And Cressida

Immediately following each quotation is a reference to the character, play, act and scene from which it originates.

Direct reading of the plays and cross-referencing with other works was complete enough to discover, for example, in Mr. Bartlett's <u>A Complete Concordance of Shakespeare</u>, (St. Martin's Press, 1966) that the word "breakfast" was cited as definitively occurring fifteen times. Now anyone assembling a complete concordance would hardly want to overlook a Shakespearean breakfast of all things. Right? (According to the preface of this work, this concordance was begun in 1876.) But, there was one breakfast, yet unlisted!

Falstaff, in
I Henry IV, Act 3, Scene 3:

Hostess,
my breakfast; come.

Imagine the quickening pulse in *a peppercorn* (Falstaff, I Henry IV, 3,3) as myself, who discovered his own breakfast count to be one better than an authoritative source he was cross-referencing with at the time! The joy in finding that "missing breakfast" left me juggling my viands without end.

After this "liberation of the viands" and playing host to thousands of viandular quotations neatly printed and then scissored into 2 x 5 inch strips, came the awesome task of selection, stylization and arrangement for the Chefspearean Classifications. Careful attention was given to this task in order to create a body of information capable of sustaining palpable interest without becoming dry or concordance-like for popular readership. Typical of Chefspearean stylization is the arrangement of quotations in such a way as to create the semblance of near-to-flowing dialogue among the diverse viandular sources on each page. I pray this task has been accomplished.

The glossary I hope will do what glossaries are suppose to do. For additional insight one can consult <u>A Shakespeare Glossary</u>, (Oxford University Press, 1963) by (who else), Mr. C.T. Onions, available at most libraries.

And finally, no attempts have been made to animate any secondary (sometimes risque) meaning given to what otherwise are innocent viandular quotations. If one favors extra spice, let imagination be the seasoning.

Whether you are perusing for epicurean insights, literary gems, or both, the opportunity to ignite the culinary fancy and not only sow the seeds for an equally worthy sequel, but also to significantly contribute in nurturing the first *pan-cultural cuisine* to exist in the world (described on pgs. 164-168) are placed at your feet by this cook.

In closing, I hope this book in part, will play its own role on the world's stage in brightening our awareness and appreciation for the beauty, sweetness, healthfulness and possibilities of the Shakespearean viands; reminding us, that long before the prosaic combinations of nachos and cheese and pizza and beer had entwined with our lives, there were and will remain to be, viands in verse and Butter In The Bard. *A good digestion to you all.* (Cardinal Wolsey, Henry VIII, 1,4). Until our next repast, I remain,

Dessertfully yours,

Chef Bob Bernoskie

A plague O' these pickle herring.
(Sir Toby Belch, Twelfth Night, 1,5)

If you have been led to believe this book is the story of a wine vintner and beer-drinking butcher from Ashford who on the feast of Lupercal forsake their vineyards, meads, slaughter-house, happy hours and grand liquor for barnyard activity among sundry animals, giddy geese and a barrow of offal all the while preoccupied with eating beef, mustard, partridge wings, finch eggs, garlic and cheese in a windmill far while in the spiced Indian air by night a gossiping, cherry-nosed maiden munching chestnuts and prunes carried in a strawberry spotted handkerchief prepares gourmet salads with Egyptian grapes and the ripest mulberries to be served in unwholesome dishes all for three pence to stern untutor'd churls and other products of blameful beds who exhibit insatiable appetites for dinners, suppers and breakfasts with a serving ratio of eight roasted boars, flap-jacks and puddings to but twelve persons mumbling all sorts of viandular observations to a wine vintner and butcher from Ashford running with a blackened cauldron and pursued by three old hags and a group of thespians named after abject orts and homeboy cates this is not what this book is about.

— The Publisher

CHEFSPEARE *

The Culinary

Classifications

* Chefspeare, defined, page 164

I

Love's Labour's Sauc'd

Bounteous Beverages

Bring me to the party.

Stephano, The Tempest, 3,2

To all, and him, we thirst.

Macbeth, Macbeth, 3,4

A stoop of wine Maria!

Sir Toby, Twelfth Night, 2,3

Wine, wine, wine!

First Servant, Coriolanus, 4,5

Thank
God, and the good wine.

York, II Henry VI, 2,3

Taste of your wine, and see what cates you have.

Talbot, I Henry VI, 2,3

'Twere as good a deed as to drink
when a man's a-hungry.

Sir Andrew, Twelfth Night, 2,3

I am a rogue, if I drunk to-day.

Falstaff, I Henry IV, 2,4

All shall eat and drink on my score.

Jack Cade, II Henry VI, 4,2

Dost thou thirst?
Pistol, Henry V, 5,1

Here's a pot of good double-
beer, neighbour.
Third Neighbor, II Henry VI, 2,3

O most courageous day! O most happy hour.
Quince, A Midsummer Night's Dream, 4,2

Fill the cup, and let it come;
I'll pledge you a mile to the bottom.
Silence, II Henry IV, 5,3

Go fetch me a quart of sack.
Falstaff, The Merry Wives Of Windsor, 3,5

Give master Bardolph some wine.
Shallow, II Henry IV, 5,3

A cup of wine, that's brisk and fine,
And drink unto the leman mine.
And a merry heart lives long-a.
Silence, II Henry IV, 5,3

I pray, come and
crush a cup of wine.
Servant, Romeo And Juliet, 1,2

And then we shall repent each drop.
Constance, King John, 2,1

Omit no happy hour.

King Henry, Henry V, 1,2

Go brew me a
pottle of sack finely.

Falstaff, The Merry Wives Of Windsor, 3,5

You love sack, and so do I.

Falstaff, The Merry Wives Of Windsor, 2,1

I drink unto your grace.

Prince John, II Henry IV, 4,2

Tell not me; — when the butt is out we
will drink water; not a drop before.

Stephano, The Tempest, 3,2

You have stayed me in a happy hour.

Beatrice, Much Ado About Nothing, 4,1

Whereto thy tongue a party-verdict gave.

King Richard, Richard II, 1,3

My heart is thirsty for that noble pledge.

Cassius, Julius Caesar, 4,3

I do suspect this trash to be a party.

Iago, Othello, 5,1

And here, neighbour, here's a cup
of charneco.

Second Neighbour, II Henry VI, 2,3

You would drink freely.

Westmoreland, II Henry IV, 4,2

Salisbury, cheer thy spirit with this comfort.

Talbot, I Henry VI, 1,4

The duke will drink under this tree.

Amiens, As You Like It, 2,5

He calls for wine.

Gremio, The Taming Of The Shrew, 3,2

A cup of wine, Sir?

Davy, II Henry IV, 5,3

I have drunk too
much sack at supper.

Shallow, II Henry IV, 5,3

How he hath drunk, he cracks his gorge.

Leontes, The Winter's Tale, 2,1

Lord Timon's happy hours are done and past.

First Stranger, Timon of Athens, 3,2

We stand a special party.
> Marcus, Titus Andronicus, 1,1

I charge and
command, that, of the city's cost, the pissing-
conduit run nothing but claret wine this first year
of our reign.
> Jack Cade, II Henry VI, 4,6

We drink this standing-bowl of wine to him.
> Simonides, Pericles, 2,4

Set a deep glass of Rhenish wine on the
contrary casket.
> Portia, The Merchant Of Venice, 1,2

Abstinence engenders maladies.
> Biron, Love's Labour's Lost, 4,3

I shall drink in pipe-
wine first with him.
> Ford, The Merry Wives of Windsor, 3,2

On the ice.
> Horatio, Hamlet, 1,1

And shall our quick blood, spirited with wine,
Seem frosty?
> Constable F., Henry V, 3,5

Upon my party, I'll revolt.
> Marcius, Coriolanus, 1,1

These clothes are good enough to drink
in, and so be these boots too.
> Sir Toby, Twelfth Night, 1,3

Go with me to
the alehouse.
> Launce, The Two Gentlemen Of Verona, 2,5

Drinking will undo you.
> Maria, Twelfth Night, 1,3

A quart of ale is a dish for a king.
> Autolycus, The Winter's Tale, 4,2

No discrace shall fall you for refusing.
> Enobarbus, Antony and Cleopatra 3,7

I have drunk but one cup to-night.
> Cassio, Othello, 2,3

Come, leave your drinking.
> Salisbury, II Henry VI, 2,3

Drink, and pray for
me, I pray for you.
> Peter, II Henry VI, 2,3

My prayers on the adverse party.
> Duchess, Richard III, 4,4

Why should hard-favour'd grief be lodg'd in thee,
When triumph is become an alehouse guest?
Queen, Richard II, 5,1

Would I were in an alehouse in London!
I would give all my fame for a pot of ale.
Boy, Henry V, 3,2

And, once again, a pot o' the smallest ale.
Sly, The Taming Of The Shrew, Induction, 2

She brews good ale.
Speed, The Two Gentlemen Of Verona, 3,1

I'll drink to her, as long as there is a passage in
my throat and drink in Illyria.
Sir Toby, Twelfth Night, 1,3

She will often praise her liquor.
Speed, The Two Gentlemen Of Verona, 3,1

Let me
see thee, froth and lime.
Host, The Merry Wives Of Windsor, 1,3

In thy vats our cares be drown'd.
Enobarbus, Antony And Cleopatra, 2,7

I drink to you.
Timon, Timon Of Athens, 1,2

Will 't please your lordship drink a
cup of sack?

First Servant, The Taming Of The Shrew,
Induction, 2

Set me the stoups of wine upon that
table.

King, Hamlet, 5,2

If
I were a huge man, I should fear to drink at
meals;
Lest they should spy my windpipe's dangerous
notes:
Great men should drink with harness on their
throats.

Apemantus, Timon Of Athens, 1,2

Hell is empty,
And all the devils are here.

Ariel, The Tempest, 1,2

Thy flatters yet wear silk, drink wine, lie soft.

Apemantus, Timon Of Athens, 4,3

I have kept me from the cup.

Menecrates, Antony And Cleopatra, 2,7

I'll not drink.

Cleopatra, Antony And Cleopatra, 5,2

We'll teach you to drink deep ere you depart.

Hamlet, Hamlet, 1,2

There's not the meanest spirit on our party.

Paris, Troilus and Cressida, 2,2

Cup us, till the world go round;
Cup us, till the world go round!
>   Caesar; Antony; Pompey; Lepidus;
>   Agrippa; Mecaenas; Enobarbus;
>   Menas; and other captains,
>   Antony And Cleopatra, 2,7

The rascal people, thirsting.
>   Second Messenger, II Henry VI, 4,4

The red wine first must rise
In their fair cheeks, my lord; then we shall have
      'em
>   Lord Sands, Henry VIII, 1,4

Party for the gain thereof.
>   Catesby, Richard III, 3,2

Give me some drink.
>   Cardinal Beaufort, II Henry VI, 3,3

Bring in banquet quickly; wine
enough
Cleopatra's health to drink.
>   Enobarbus, Antony And Cleopatra, 1,2

Give me a cup of sack.
>   Falstaff, I Henry IV, 2,4

I drink to you in a cup of sack.
>   First Neighbor, II Henry VI, 2,3

And with mine eyes I'll drink the words you send,
Though ink be made of gall.
>   Posthumus, Cymbeline, 1,1

46

I drink to the general joy of the whole table.
Macbeth, Macbeth, 3,4

An intelligent party.
Edmund, King Lear, 3,5

They shall taste our comfort.
Cymbeline, Cymbeline, 5,5

Fair thoughts and happy hours attend on you!
Lorenzo, The Merchant of Venice, 3,4

I think you all have drunk of Circe's cup.
Duke, The Comedy Of Errors, 5,1

Where should they
Find this grand liquor that hath gilded 'em?
Alonso, The Tempest, 5,1

The vines of France and milk of Burgundy,
Strive to be interess'd.
King Lear, King Lear, 1,1

Both have I spill'd.
Exton, Richard II, 5,5

It was excess of wine that set him on.
King Henry, Henry V, 2,2

What a beard of the
general's cut, and a horrid suit of the camp, will
do among foaming bottles, and ale-washed wits, is
wonderful to be thought on!
> Gower, Henry V, 3,6

All your southern gentlemen in arms upon his party.
> Scroop, Richard II, 3,2

Our legions are brim-full, our cause is ripe.
> Brutus, Julius Caesar, 4,3

They have made him drink alms-drink.
> First Servant, Antony And Cleopatra, 2,7

Might they not stop a beer-barrel?
> Hamlet, Hamlet, 5,1

Our party may well meet.
> Bastard, King John, 5,1

I will
make it felony, to drink small beer.
> Jack Cade, II Henry VI, 4,2

Win the noble Brutus to our party.
> Cinna, Julius Caesar, 1,3

To the king's party there's no going.
> Belarius, Cymbeline, 4,4

Good friends, go in, and taste some
wine with me.

Caesar, Julius Caesar, 2,2

I saw our party.

Messenger, Coriolanus, 1,6

I, that was wash'd to death with fulsome wine.

Ghost, Richard III, 5,3

I should show
What party I do follow.

Oswald, King Lear, 4,5

I am known to be a humorour patrician,
and one that loves a cup of hot wine.

Menenius, Coriolanus, 2,1

Will I with wine and wassail so convince.

Lady Macbeth, Macbeth, 1,7

I'll heat his blood with Greekish wine
to-night.

Achilles, Troilus And Cressida, 5,1

For then both parties nobly are subdued.

Archbishop, II Henry IV, 4,2

Wine loved I deeply.

Edgar, King Lear, 3,4

Lucius, a bowl of wine.

Brutus, Julius Caesar, 4,3

Let my liver rather heat with wine.

Gratiano, The Merchant Of Venice, 1,1

'Tis fit you make strong party.

Cominius, Coriolanus, 3,2

Fill me some wine.

Lucullus, Timon Of Athens, 3,1

Fill me a bowl of wine.

King Richard, Richard III, 5,3

Give me a bowl
of wine.

Brutus, Julius Caesar, 4,3

Have we no wine here?

Coriolanus, Coriolanus, 1,9

To Burdeaux.

William Lucy, I Henry VI, 4,3

II

The Taming
Of
The Stew

Meat, It Does a Corpus Good!

Meat was made for mouths.
Marcius, Coriolanus, 1,1

What say you to a piece of beef, and mustard?
Grumio, The Taming Of The Shrew, 4,3

I am a great eater of beef, and I
Believe that does harm to my wit.
Sir Andrew, Twelfth Night, 1,3

Here's my money for my meat.
Imogen, Cymbeline, 3,6

'T is burnt; and so is all the meat:
where is the rascal cook?
Petruchio, The Taming Of The Shrew, 4,1

I scorn thy meat; 't would choke me,
for I should ne'er flatter thee.
Apemantus, Timon Of Athens, 1,2

Have I lived to be carried
in a basket, like a barrow of butcher's offal.
Falstaff, The Merry Wives Of Windsor, 3,5

Sir, I will eat no meat.
Cleopatra, Julius Caesar, 5,2

Roast me in sulphur!
Othello, Othello, 5,2

But mice and rats, and such small deer,
    Have been Tom's food for seven long year.
        Edgar, King Lear, 3,4

He is a very epicure.
        Antony, Antony And Cleopatra, 2,7

Feeds from home.
        Adriana, The Comedy Of Errors, 2,1

The king he is hunting the deer.
        Biron, Love's Labour's Lost, 4,3

Stew'd in corruption.
        Hamlet, Hamlet, 3,4

Unwholesome food, they say.
        Boy, Henry V, 2,3

Thou hast no feeling of it.
        Costard, Love's Labour's Lost, 3,1

Thou shalt be whipp'd with wire, and stew'd in
    brine.
        Cleopatra, Antony And Cleopatra, 2,5

Moody food.
        Cleopatra, Antony And Cleopatra, 2,5,

We have a hot venison pasty to dinner;
come gentlemen.
Mistress Page, The Merry Wives Of Windsor, 1,1

Sit down and feed, and welcome to our table.
Duke S., As You Like It, 2,7

I thank you for my venison.
Page, The Merry Wives Of Windsor, 1,1

I think the meat wants...
Basting.
Dromio S., The Comedy Of Errors, 2,2

Make not a city feast of it,
to let your meat cool.
Timon, Timon Of Athens, 3,6

I cannot abide the smell of hot meat.
Slender, The Merry Wives Of Windsor, 1,1

Here, take away this dish.
Petruchio, The Taming Of the Shrew, 4,3

A knave; a rascal; an eater of broken meats.
Earl of Kent, King Lear, 2,2

Ay, she quickly pooped him; she made
him roast-meat for worms.
Boult, Pericles, 4,2

Upon what meat does this our Caesar feed,
That he is grown so great?

Cassius, Julius Caesar, 1,2

Thou false deluding
slave,
That feed'st me with the very name of meat.

Katharina, The Taming Of The Shrew, 4,3

It is meat and drink to me to see a
clown.

Touchstone, As You Like It, 5,1

Seest how diligent I am,
To dress thy meat myself.

Petruchio, The Taming Of The Shrew, 4,3

Touch the meat.

Katharina, The Taming Of The Shrew, 4,3

Pr'ythee, let my meat make thee
silent.

Timon, Timon Of Athens, 1,2

He might have broiled and eaten him too.

Second Servant, Coriolanus, 4,5

Beastly feeder.

Archbishop, II Henry IV, 1,3

Feed his humor.

Publius, Titus Andronicus, 4,3

Look to the bak'd meats, good Angelica:
Spare not for cost.
>> Capulet, Romeo And Juliet, 4,4

But one meal on everyday.
>> Biron, Love's Labour's Lost, 1,1

    That
roasted Manningtree ox with the pudding in his
belly.
>> Prince Henry, I Henry IV, 2,4

We'll fall to it with our teeth.
>> First Servant, I Henry VI, 3,1

We shall feed like oxen at a stall.
>> Worcester, I Henry IV, 5,2

High feeding.
>> Northumberland, II Henry IV, 1,1

Porridge after meat!
>> Pandarus, Troilus And Cressida, 1,2

Highly fed.
>> Clown, All's Well That Ends Well, 2,2

We now are full.
>> Troilus, Troilus And Cressida, 2,2

Eat strange flesh.

Caesar, Antony And Cleopatra, 1,4

Eat a crocodile? I'll do it.

Hamlet, Hamlet, 5,1

Slice, I say!

Nym, The Merry Wives Of Windsor, 1,1

We are prepared.

Austria, King John, 2,1

She eat no meat to-day, nor none shall eat.

Petruchio, The Taming Of The Shrew, 4,1

Food and diet.

Horatio, Hamlet, 1,1

What you want in
meat we'll have in drink.

Davy, II Henry IV, 5,3

These English are shrewdly out
of beef.

Orleans, Henry V, 3,7

Longing as I said for prunes.

Pompey, Measure For Measure, 2,1

III

The Merry Chicks
Of
Windsor

Poetic Poultry and Other Fowl Mete

Good capon.
> Jaques, As You Like It, 2,7

Breast of heaven.
> Cassius, Julius Caesar, 1,3

The poor chicken should be sure of death.
> Queen Margaret, II Henry VI, 3,1

Troubled breast.
> Pembroke, King John, 4,2

All my pretty chickens.
> Macduff, Macbeth, 4,3

Your legs should do it.
> King, Love's Labour's Lost, 5,2

To all that fortune, death, and danger dare,
Even for an egg-shell.
> Hamlet, Hamlet, 4,4

Kate will be my hen.
> Petruchio, The Taming Of The Shrew, 2,1

The best feather of our wing.
> Iachimo, Cymbeline, 1,6

Eggs, sir?

Bardolph, The Merry Wives Of Windsor, 3,5

I would break a thousand.

Edward, III Henry VI, 1,2

I have cut the egg i' th'
middle, and eat up the meat.

Fool, King Lear, 1,4

Thou'dst shiver'd like an egg.

Edgar, King Lear, 4,6

Nuncle, give me an egg, and I'll give thee two
crowns.

Fool, King Lear, 1,4

Thy head is as full of quarrels,
as an egg is full of meat; and yet thy head hath
been beaten as addle as an egg, for quarrelling.

Mercutio, Romeo And Juliet, 3,1

They say we are
Almost as like as eggs.

Leontes, The Winter's Tale, 1,2

But what we do determine oft we break.

Hamlet, Hamlet, 3,2

Some trick not worth an egg, shall grow dear
friends.

Coriolanus, Coriolanus, 4,4

Hang me
up by the heels for a rabbit-sucker, or a poulter's
hare.
                    Falstaff, I Henry IV, 2,4

He will steal, sir, an egg out of a cloister.
                    Parolles, All's Well That Ends Well, 4,3

        And his shipping, —
Poor ingnorant baubles! — on our terrible seas,
Like egg-shells mov'd upon their surges, crack'd
As easily 'gainst our rocks.
                    Queen, Cymbeline, 3,1

        Mine honest
        friend,
Will you take eggs for money?
                    Hermione, The Winter's Tale, 1,2

Ye giddy goose.
                    Lady Percy, I Henry IV, 3,1

If you love an addle egg as well as you
love an idle head, you would eat chickens i' the
shell.
                    Cressida, Troilus And Cressida, 1,2

        I'll never
Be such a gosling to obey instinct.
                    Coriolanus, Coriolanus, 5,3

She's e'en setting on water to scald such
chickens as you are.
                    Fool, Timon Of Athens, 2,2

Breast to breast.
                    King Henry, III Henry VI, 2,5

Finch egg!
Thersites, Troilus And Cressida, 5,1

Break it to our hope.
Macbeth, Macbeth, 5,8

I have no pheasant, cock
nor hen.
Shepherd, The Winter's Tale, 4,3

The turkies in my pannier
are quite starved.
First Carrier, I Henry IV, 2,1

They have left their viands behind.
Sebastian, The Tempest, 3,3

I eat the air, promise-crammed: you cannot feed capons so.
Hamlet, Hamlet, 3,2

The capon burns.
Dromio E., The Comedy Of Errors, 1,2

Anything so overdone is from the purpose of playing.
Hamlet, Hamlet, 3,2

I
can suck melancholy out of a song, as a weazel
sucks eggs.
Jaques, As You Like It, 2,5

Steals her capon's leg. O, 't is a foul thing.

Launce, The Two Gentlemen Of Verona, 4,4

Seeking the food he eats
And pleased with what he gets.

Song, As You Like It, 2,5

In fair round belly with good capon lin'd.

Jaques, As You Like It, 2,7

          I fear
Thou play'dst most foully for 't.

Banquo, Macbeth, 3,1

You can carve. Break up this capon.

Princess, Love's Labour's Lost, 4,1

Jack, how agrees the devil and thee
about thy soul, that thou soldest him on Good-
Friday last, for a cup of Madeira, and a cold
capon's leg?

Poins, I Henry IV, 1,2

I would nor refuse.

Portia, Merchant Of Venice, 1,2

Lord have mercy on thee for a hen.

Lafeu, All's Well That Ends Well, 2,3

Such things become the hatch and brood of time.

Warwick, II Henry IV, 3,1

There's a partridge' wing saved, for the
fool will eat no supper that night. [music within]
Beatrice, Much Ado About Nothing, 2,1

An honest fellow enough, and one that loves quails.
Thersites, Troilus and Cressida, 5,1

Some pigeons,
Davy; a couple of short-legged hens; a joint of
mutton.
Shallow, II Henry IV, 5,1

I have here a dish of doves, that I would
bestow upon your worship.
Gobbo, The Merchant Of Venice, 2,2

I smell some l'envoy, some goose.
Costard, Love's Labour's Lost, 3,1

Eyes do you see? How can it be? O dainty duck!
Pyramus, A Midsummer Night's Dream, 5,1

For our kitchens we kill the fowl of season.
Isabella, Measure For Measure, 2,2

He hath bid me to a calf's head and a capon.
Claudio, Much Ado About Nothing, 5,1

O, break my heart.
Juliet, Romeo And Juliet, 3,2

IV

The Culinary Couplets

Biron:	White-handed mistress, one sweet word with thee.
Princess:	Honey, and milk, and sugar; there is three.

Love's Labour's Lost, 5,2

Beatrice:	Will you not eat your word?
Benedick:	With no sauce that can be devised to it: I protest.

Much Ado About Nothing, 4,1

Beatrice:	Do not swear by it, and eat it.
Benedick:	I will swear by it, that you love me; and I will make him eat it, that says, I love not you.

Much Ado About Nothing, 4,1

Gaoler:	Come, sir, are you ready for death?
Posthumus:	Over-roasted rather; ready long ago.

Cymbeline, 5,4

Gaoler:	Hanging is the word, sir; if you be ready for that, you are well cooked.
Posthumus:	So, if I prove a good repast to the spectators, the dish pays the shot.

Cymbeline, 5,4

Julia:	Is't near dinner-time?
Lucetta:	I would it were;
	That you might kill your stomach on your meat,
	And not upon your maid.

The Two Gentlemen Of Verona, 1,2

Cassius:	Will you dine with me to-morrow?
Casca:	Ay, if I be alive, and your mind hold,
	and your dinner worth the eating.

Julius Caesar, 1,2

Armado:	Villain, thou shalt fast for thy offences
	ere thou be pardoned.
Costard:	Well, sir, I hope, when I do it, I shall
	do it on a full stomach.

Love's Labour's Lost, 1,2

| Sir Evans: | Focative is caret. |
| Mistress Q: | And that's a good root. |

The Merry Wives Of Windsor, 4,1

King:	You
	shall fast a week with bran and water.
Costard:	I had rather pray a month with mutton and
	porridge.

Love's Labour's Lost, 1,1

Orleans:	He's of the colour of the nutmeg.
Dauphin:	And of the heat of the ginger.

Henry V, 3,7

Biron:	A lemon.
Longaville:	Stuck with cloves.

Love's Labour's Lost, 5,2

Timon:	Where feed'st thou o'days, Apemantus?
Apemantus:	Where my stomach finds meat; or rather, where I eat it.

Timon Of Athens, 4,3

Peto:
Item, a capon .... 2s. 2d.
Item, Sauce .... 4d.
Item, Sack, two gallons .... 5s. 8d.
Item, Anchovies, and sack after supper .. 2s. 6d.
Item, Bread .... ob.

Prince Henry:
    O monstrous! but one half-penny-worth of bread to this intolerable deal of sack!

I Henry IV, 2,4

V

Twelfth Bite;
Or
What You Wilt

Salads/Fruits and Veggies in Verse

One said there were no sallets.
> Hamlet, Hamlet, 2,2

Now the word sallet must serve me
to feed on.
> Jack Cade, II Henry VI, 4,10

On a brick-wall have I
climbed into this garden, to see if I can eat
grass, or pick a sallet another while, which is not
amiss to cool a man's stomach this hot weather.
> Jack Cade, II Henry VI, 4,10

We may pick a thousand salads, ere we light on
such another herb.
> Lafeu, All's Well That Ends Well, 4,5

My salad days:
When I was green in judgment.
> Cleopatra, Antony And Cleopatra, 1,5

We'll come dress you.
> Mrs. Page, The Merry Wives Of Windsor, 4,2

Tut, Tut; good enough to toss.
> Falstaff, I Henry IV, 4,2

⊱ FRUITS ⊰

We will go walk a little in the orchard.
> Baptista, The Taming Of The Shrew, 2,1

Nay, you shall see mine orchard; where,
in an arbour, we will eat a last year's pippin of
my own graffing, with a dish of carraways, and so
forth.
> Shallow, II Henry IV, 5,3

Witness the loving kiss I give the fruit.
> Gloucester, III Henry VI, 5,7

     There's pippins and
cheese to come.
> Sir Evans, The Merry Wives Of Windsor, 1,2

There is a dish of leather-coats for you.
> Davy, II Henry IV, 5,3

Feed him with apricocks, and dewberries,
With purple grapes, green figs, and mulberries.
> Titania, A Midsummer Night's Dream, 3,2

     And
longing — saving your honour's reverence — for
stewed prunes.
> Pompey, Measure For Measure, 2,1

With thy grapes our hairs be crown'd.
> Enobarbus, Antony And Cleopatra, 2,7

When roasted crabs hiss in the bowl.
> Winter, Love's Labour's Lost, 5,2

The heathen philosopher, when he had a desire to eat a grape, would open his lips when he put it into his mouth, meaning thereby, that grapes were made to eat, and lips to open.

Touchstone, As You Like It, 5,1

Vines, with clust'ring bunches growing;
Plants, with goodly burden bowing.

Ceres, The Tempest, 4,1

The juice of Egypt's grape shall moist this lip.

Cleopatra, Antony And Cleopatra, 5,2

Give grandame kingdom, and it grandame will
Give it a plum, a cherry, and a fig.

Constance, King John, 2,1

He brings you figs.

Guard, Julius Caesar, 5,2

A fig for Peter.

Horner, II Henry VI, 2,3

The fig of Spain!

Pistol, Henry V, 2,3

Virtue! A fig!

Iago, Othello, 1,3

Best to preserve it.

Antony, Antony And Cleopatra, 3,4

Foolish curs, that run winking into the
mouth of a Russian bear, and have their heads
crushed like rotten apples!
>> Orleans, Henry V, 3,7

They might have liv'd to bear, and he to taste,
The fruits of duty.
>> Gardner, Richard II, 3,4

>> I love long life better than
figs.
>> Soothsayer, Antony And Cleopatra, 1,2

Where in the purlicus of this forest stands
A sheep-cote, fenc'd about with olive-trees?
>> Oliver, As You Like It, 4,3

To that vineyard is a planched gate.
>> Isabella, Measure For Measure, 4,2

>> Our vineyards, fallows, meads, and hedges,
Defective in their natures, grow to wildness.
>> Duke B., Henry V, 5,2

O'fie! 'tis an unweeded garden,
That grows to seed.
>> Hamlet, Hamlet, 1,2

Hang there like fruit, my soul,
Till the tree die!
>> Posthumus, Cymbeline, 5,5

>> Let us quit all,
And give our vineyards to a barbarous people.
>> Constable F., Henry V, 3,5

My wife desired some damsons.
Simpcox, II Henry VI, 2,1

Kate, like the hazel-twig,
Is straight, and slender; and as brown in hue,
As hazel-nuts, and sweeter than the kernels.
Petruchio, The Taming Of The Shrew, 2,1

Her inkle, silk, twin with rubied cherry.
Gower, Pericles, 4,6

In her days every man shall eat in safety
Under his own vine, what he plants.
Cranmer, Henry VIII, 5,4

Sometime lurk I in a gossip's bowl,
In very likeness of a roasted crab;
And, when she drinks, against her lips I bob.
Puck, A Midsummer Night's Dream, 2,1

Laugh upon the apple of her eye?
King, Love's Labour's Lost, 5,2

Go to sir; you were beaten in Italy for
picking a kernel out of a pomegranate.
Lafeu, All's Well That Ends Well, 2,4

Where hast thou been preserv'd?
Hermione, The Winter's Tale, 5,3

Your old virginity, is like one of our French
withered pears; it looks ill, it eats drily; marry,
't is a withered pear.
Parolles, All's Well That Ends Well, 1,1

King Edwards fruit, true heir
to the English Crown.

Queen Elizabeth, III Henry VI, 4,4

Like the fruit of such a goodly tree.

King Henry, III Henry VI, 5,6

I may beg; —
four pound of prunes, and as many of raisins o'
the sun.

Clown, The Winter's Tale, 4,2

Give me
Water with berries in 't.

Caliban, The Tempest, 1,2

A dish of stewed prunes.

Slender, The Merry Wives Of Windsor, 1,1

This is the fruit of rashness!

Gloucester, Richard III, 2,1

I marvel how he sped.

Alencon, I Henry VI, 2,1

What the devil hast thou brought
there? apple-Johns? thou knowest sir John
cannot endure an apple-John.

First Drawer, II Henry IV, 2,4

                    Sir, your queen
Desires your visitation, and to be
Acquainted with this stranger; 't is as like you
As cherry is to cherry.
> Old Lady, Henry VIII, 5,1

My news shall be the fruit to that great feast.
> Polonius, Hamlet, 2,2

Something is rotten in the state of
Denmark.
> Marcellus, Hamlet, 1,4

A nut, a cherry-stone.
> Dromio E., The Comedy Of Errors, 4,3

There's small choice
in rotten apples.
> Hortensio, The Taming Of The Shrew, 1,1

Not this rotten orange.
> Claudio, Much Ado About Nothing, 4,1

Your fruitful brain.
> Rosaline, Love's Labour's Lost, 5,2

Fair fruit in an unwholesome dish,
Are like to rot untasted.
> Agamemnon, Troilus And Cressida, 2,3

        A fruit-dish, a dish of some three-pence, — your
honours have seen such dishes.
> Pompey, Measure For Measure, 2,1

The strawberry grows underneath the
nettle,
And wholesome berries thrive and ripen best,
Neighbour'd by fruit of baser quality.

Bishop of Ely, Henry V, 1,1

I saw good strawberries in your garden.

Buckingham, Richard III, 3,4

Have you not seen a handkerchief
Spotted with strawberries in your wife's hand?

Iago, Othello, 3,3

Walk here i' the orchard, I'll bring her
straight.

Pandarus, Troilus And Cressida, 3,2

O, will you eat no grapes, my royal fox?

Lafeu, All's Well That Ends Well, 2,1

There's one grape yet.

Lafeu, All's Well That Ends Well, 2,3

Distill'd almost to jelly.

Horatio, Hamlet, 1,2

I have sent for these strawberries.

Bishop of Ely, Richard III, 3,4

God bless it and preserve it.

Fluellen, Henry V, 4,7

Three crabbed months had sour'd themselves to
    death.
        Hermione, The Winter's Tale, 1,2

    The sun looks pale,
Killing their fruit with frowns?
        Constable F., Henry V, 3,5

Thy mother took into her blameful bed
Some stern untutor'd churl, and nobel stock
Was graft with crab-tree slip; whose fruit thou art.
        Warwick, II Henry VI, 3,2

I pr'thee let me bring thee where crabs grow.
        Caliban, The Tempest, 2,2

                      [will not
We have some old crab-trees here at home, that
Be grafted to your relish.
        Menenius, Coriolanus, 2,1

    We at time of year
Do wound the bark, the skin of our fruit-trees;
Lest, being over-proud in sap and blood,
With too much riches it confound itself.
        Gardener, Richard II, 3,4

    If reasons were as plenty
as blackberries, I would give no man a reason
upon compulsion, I.
        Falstaff, I Henry IV, 2,4

    Humble as the ripest mulberry
That will not hold the handling.
        Volumnia, Coriolanus, 3,2

She took the fruits of my advice.
        Polonius, Hamlet, 2,2

His lordship is walk'd forth into the
orchard.
Porter, II Henry IV, 1,1

His passion is so ripe, it needs must break.
Salisbury, King John, 4,2

Taste the fruit of yon celestial tree.
Pericles, Pericles, 1,1

Those happy smilets,
That play'd on her ripe lip.
A Gentleman, King Lear, 4,3

Thy lips, those kissing cherries, tempting grow!
Demetrius, A Midsummer Night's Dream, 3,2

Two lovely berries moulded on one stem.
Helena, A Midsummer Night's Dream, 3,2

Peace puts forth her olive everywhere.
Westmoreland, II Henry IV, 4,4

There's a medlar for thee, eat it.
Apemantus, Timon Of Athens, 4,3

So we grew together,
Like to a double cherry, seeming parted.
Helena, A Midsummer Night's Dream, 3,2

I
bruised my shin the other day with playing at
sword and dagger with a master of fence, three
veneys for a dish of stewed prunes.

> Slender, The Merry Wives Of Windsor, 1,1

This cherry nose.

> Thisbe, A Midsummer Night's Dream, 5,1

'T was in the Bunch of Grapes.

> Pompey, Measure For Measure, 2,1

Pinch the maids as blue as bilberry.

> Pistol, The Merry Wives Of Windsor, 5,5

The bloom that promiseth a mighty fruit.

> Elinor, King John, 2,2

All the other gifts appertinent to man,
as the malice of this age shapes them, are not
worth a gooseberry.

> Falstaff, II Henry IV, 1,2

An apple tart.

> Petruchio, The Taming Of The Shrew, 4,3

Blessed fig's end!

> Iago, Othello, 2,1

Poor market-folks, that come to sell their corn.
La Pucelle, I Henry VI, 3,2

Good morrow, gallants! want ye corn for
bread?
La Pucelle, I Henry VI, 3,2

We'll have corn at
our own price.
First Citizen, Coriolanus, 1,1

Friends, Romans, countrymen, lend me
your ears.
Antony, Julius Caesar, 3,2

The gods sent not corn for the rich men only.
Marcius, Coriolanus, 1,1

First thrash the corn, then after burn the straw.
Demetrius, Titus Andronicus, 2,3

Her foes shake like a field of beaten corn.
Cranmer, Henry VIII, 5,4

What's past and what's to come is strew'd with
husks.
Agamemnon, Troilus And Cressida, 4,5

He weeds the corn.
> Longaville, Love's Labour's Lost, 1,1

His eyes were green as leeks.
> Thisbe, A Midsummer Night's Dream, 5,1

When he was naked, he was, for all the world, like
a forked radish, with a head fantastically carved
upon it with a knife.
> Falstaff, II Henry IV, 3,2

And I, an ass, am onion-ey'd: for shame.
> Enobarbus, Antony And Cleopatra, 4,2

His well-proportion'd beard made rough and
  rugged,
Like to the summer's corn by tempest lodg'd.
> Suffolk, II Henry VI, 3,2

How like, methought, I then was to this kernel,
This squash, this gentleman.
> Hermione, The Winter's Tale, 1,2

But his neat cookery! he cut our roots in
characters.
> Guiderius, Cymbeline, 4,2

Mine eyes smell onions, I shall weep
anon.
> Lafeu, All's Well That Ends Well, 5,3

Have we eaten on the insane root,
That takes the reason prisoner?
> Banquo, Macbeth, 1,3

What rhubarb?
> Macbeth, Macbeth, 5,4

Let the sky rain potatoes.
> Falstaff, The Merry Wives Of Windsor, 5,5

To rain a shower of commanded tears,
An onion will do well for such a shift.
> First Player, The Taming Of The Shrew,
> Induction, Scene I

For the elegancy, facility, and golden cadence of poesy,
caret.
> Holofernes, Love's Labour's Lost, 4,2

Why droops my lord, like over-ripen'd
corn.
> Duchess G., II Henry VI, 1,2

I am qualmish at the smell of leek.
> Pistol, Henry V, 5,1

I pray you, fall
to; if you can mock a leek, you can eat a leek.
> Fluellen, Henry V, 5,1

Can you eat roots, and drink cold water?
> Timon, Timon Of Athens, 5,1

I'll make you feed on berries, and on roots.
> Aaron, Titus Andronicus, 4,2

Peas and beans are as dank here as a
dog.
> Second Carrier, I Henry IV, 2,1

Good worts! good cabbage.
> Falstaff, The Merry Wives Of Windsor, 1,1

VI

As You Spice It

Amen for All Seasonings

Sprigs of rosemary.
                Edgar, King Lear, 2,3

        Is not birth, beauty, good shape, discourse, manhood, learning, gentleness, virtue, youth, liberality, and such like, the spice and salt that seasons a man?
                Pandarus, Troilus And Cressida, 1,2

Soft! it smells most sweetly in my sense.
                Cerimon, Pericles, 3,2

In the spiced Indian air by night.
                Titania, A Midsummer Night's Dream, 2,1

Doth not rosemary and Romeo begin both with a letter?
                Nurse, Romeo And Juliet, 2,4

Sweet marjorum.
                Edgar, King Lear, 4,6

Bid Nestor bring me spices.
                Pericles, Pericles, 3,1

Hot lavender, mints, savory, marjorum.
                Perdita, The Winter's Tale, 4,3

        I have led my ragamuffins
where they are peppered.
                Falstaff, I Henry IV, 5,3

You, minion, are too saucy.

Julia, The Two Gentlemen Of Verona, 1,2

How cam'st thou in this pickle?

Alonso, The Tempest, 5,1

Sea-water shalt thou drink;

Prospero, The Tempest, 1,2

Leave in sooth. And such protest of pepper-
gingerbread.

Hotspur, I Henry IV, 3,1

This rudeness is a sauce to his good wit,
Which gives men stomach to digest his words
With better appetite.

Cassius, Julius Caesar, 1,2

Eat your victuals; come, there is sauce
for it.

Fluellen, Henry V, 5,1

I can cut a caper.

Sir Andrew, Twelfth Night, 1,3

Fortune it belches
upon us.

Cerimon, Pericles, 3,2

How tastes it?

Old Lady, Henry VIII, 2,3

He hath a garden.

Isabella, Measure For Measure, 4,1

In that nest of spicery, they shall breed
selves of themselves to your recomforture.

King Richard, Richard III, 4,4

I must have saffron, to
colour the warden pies; mace, — dates, — none,
that's out of my note; nutmegs, seven;
a race or two of ginger;

Clown, The Winter's Tale, 4,2

They call for dates and quinces in the
pastry.

Nurse, Romeo And Juliet, 4,4

There's fennel for you, and columbines:
— there's rue for you; and here's some for me:
— we may call it herb-grace o' Sundays.

Ophelia, Hamlet, 4,6

For you there's rosemary and rue; these keep
Seeming and savour all the winter long:
Grace and remembrance be to you both.

Perdita, The Winter's Tale, 4,3

There's rosemary, that's for remembrance.

Ophelia, Hamlet, 4,6

VII

Much Ado About Mutton

In The Barn of The Bard

What's this? mutton?
> Petruchio, The Taming Of The Shrew, 4,1

Give me a sword, I'll chop.
> Titus, Titus Andronicus, 3,1

I have a gammon of bacon, and two
razes of ginger.
> Second Carrier, I Henry IV, 2,1

I will use the olive with my sword.
> Alcibiades, Timon Of Athens, 5,4

A pound of man's flesh, taken from a man,
Is not so estimable, profitable neither,
As flesh of muttons, beefs, or goats.
> Shylock, The Merchant Of Venice, 1,3

There is one goat for you.
> Fluellen, Henry V, 5,1

A dish that I do love to feed upon.
> Katharina, The Taming Of The Shrew, 4,3

I can cut the mutton.
> Sir Toby, Twelfth Night, 1,3

The chopping French we do not understand.
> Duchess, Richard III, 5,3

You are no good
member of the commonwealth; for, in converting
Jews to Christians, you raise the price of pork.

Jessica, The Merchant Of Venice, 3,5

By this leek, I will most horribly revenge.

Pistol, Henry V, 5,1

Art thou of
cornish crew?

Pistol, Henry V, 4,1

Shall I keep your hogs, and eat husks
with them?

Orlando, As You Like It, 1,1

Is not the grease of a mutton as wholesome as the sweat of a man?

Touchstone, As You Like It, 3,2

The lamb entreats the butcher: where's thy knife?

Imogen, Cymbeline, 3,4

His answer was, he would unto the stews.

Percy, King Richard II, 5,3

Weke, weke! — so cries a pig prepared to the
spit.

Aaron, Titus Andronicus, 4,2

The pig falls from the spit.

Dromio E., The Comedy of Errors, 1,2

I, a lost mutton.

Speed, The Two Gentlemen Of Verona, 1,1

Wanton as youthful goats.

Vernon, I Henry IV, 4,1

Hang hog is Latin for bacon, I warrant
you.

Mistress Q., The Merry Wives Of Windsor, 4,1

To smell pork.

Shylock, The Merchant Of Venice, 1,3

The duke, I say to thee again,
would eat mutton on Fridays.

Lucio, Measure For Measure, 3,2

Feeding his own stomach.

Parolles, All's Well That Ends Well, 1,1

All vict'lers do so; what's a joint of
mutton or two, in a whole Lent?

Hostess, II Henry IV, 2,4

Let him feed.

Duke S., As You Like It, 2,7

VIII

Measure For Pleasure

Breads and Grains

Marry, they say my uncle grew so fast
That he could gnaw a crust at two hours old.
York, Richard III, 2,4

His appetite is more to bread than stone.
Duke, Measure for Measure, 1,3

That jade hath eat bread from my royal hand.
King, Richard II, 5,5

Sauc'd our broths.
Guiderius, Cymbeline, 4,2

He would mouth with
a beggar, though she smelt brown bread and
garlic.
Lucio, Measure For Measure, 3,2

He would pun thee into shivers with his
fist, as a sailor breaks a biscuit.
Thersites, Troilus And Cressida, 2,1

I will knead him.
Ajax, Troilus And Cressida, 2,3

We shall sift him.
King, Hamlet, 2,2

An honest soul, i'faith, sir; by my troth
he is, as ever broke bread
Dogberry, Much Ado About Nothing, 3,5

Ceres, most bounteous lady, thy rich leas
Of wheat, rye, barley, vetches, oats, and pease.
                    Iris, The Tempest, 4,1

        I could
munch your good dry oats.
                    Bottom, A Midsummer Night's Dream, 4,1

The gods know I speak this in hunger
for bread.
                    First Citizen, Coriolanus, 1,1

Poor fellow! never joyed since the price
of oats rose.
                    First Carrier, I Henry IV, 2,1

        The oats have
eaten the horses.
                    Grumio, The Taming Of The Shrew, 3,2

Rolls, and rolls, and rolls.
                    Fluellen, Henry V, 3,6

Lay the leaven on all.
                    Imogen, Cymbeline, 3,4

        There shall be in England
seven half-penny loaves sold for a penny.
                    Jack Cade, II Henry VI, 4,2

Some rise by sin.
                    Escalus, Measure for Measure, 2,1

Nature hath meal and bran, contempt and grace.
> Belarius, Cymbeline, 4,2

His
reasons are as two grains of wheat hid in two
bushels of chaff; you shall seek all day ere you
find them; and when you have them they are not
worth the search.
> Bassanio, The Merchant Of Venice, 1,1

Chaff and bran, chaff and bran!
> Pandarus, Troilus And Cressida, 1,2

We'll sift this matter further.
> King, All's Well That Ends Well, 5,3

Ay, to the leavening; but here's yet in
the word hereafter, the kneading, the making
of the cake, the heating of the oven, and the
baking; nay, you must stay the cooling too, or
you may chance to burn your lips.
> Pandarus, Troilus And Cressida, 1,1

A rising
sigh,
He wisheth.
> Glendower, I Henry IV, 3,1

You must tarry the leavening.
> Pandarus, Troilus And Cressida, 1,1

Go sir, rub your
chain with crumbs.
> Sir Toby, Twelfth Night, 2,3

Send
Measures of wheat to Rome.
> Pompey, Antony And Cleopatra, 2,6

We have with a leaven'd and prepared choice
proceeded to you.
Duke, Measure For Measure, 1,1

Corn to make your needy bread.
Pericles, Pericles, 1,4

I think the duke of Burgundy will fast,
Before he'll buy again at such a rate:
'T was full of darnel.
La Pucelle, I Henry VI, 3,2

Distressful bread.
King Henry, Henry V, 4,1

Eating the bitter bread of banishment.
Bolingbroke, Richard II, 3,1

He lives upon mouldy stewed prunes, and dried cakes.
Doll Tear-Sheet, II Henry IV, 2,4

He that will have a cake out of the wheat must
needs tarry the grinding.
Padnarus, Troilus And Cressida, 1,1

Those palates who, not yet two summers younger,
Must have inventions to delight the taste,
Would now be glad of bread, and beg for it.
Cleon, Pericles, 1,4

He that keeps nor crust nor crumb,
Weary of all, shall want some.
Fool, King Lear, 1,4

IX

Tide Us
And Dine W'th Us

Luncheons Were Never Mentioned

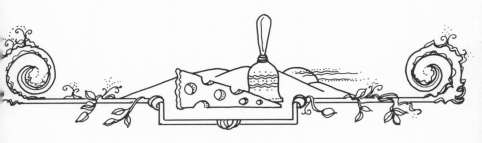

97

Hie you home to dinner.
>Dromio, The Comedy Of Errors, 1,2

Come home to dinner.
>Dromio, The Comedy Of Errors, 1,2

I shall not dine at home.
>Othello, Othello, 3,3

Where shall we dine?
>Romeo, Romeo And Juliet, 1,1

Let us to the Tiger all to dinner.
>Balthazar, The Comedy Of Errors, 3,1

With reservation of an hundred knights.
>King Lear, King Lear, 1,1

Go, I charge thee; invite them all, let in the tide
Of knaves once more; my cook and I'll provide.
>Timon, Timon Of Athens, 3,4

My knightly stomach is suffic'd.
>King John, King John, 1,1

I know they are stuff'd.
>Silvia, The Two Gentlemen Of Verona, 4,4

Where sups he? doth the old boar
feed in the old frank?
> Prince Henry, II Henry IV, 2,2

You must not know where
he sups.
> Pandarus, Troilus And Cressida, 3,1

He sups to-night with a harlotry.
> Iago, Othello, 4,2

She will indite him to some supper.
> Benrolio, Romeo And Juliet, 2,4

Shall we steal upon them,
Ned, at supper?
> Prince Henry, II Henry IV, 2,2

I desir'd him to come home to dinner.
> Dromio, The Comedy Of Errors, 2,1

Their tables were stor'd full, to glad the sight,
And not so much to feed on, as delight.
> Cleon, Pericles, 1,4

Things for the cook, sir; but I know
not what.
> First Servant, Romeo And Juliet, 4,4

The room where they supped, is too
hot.
> First Drawer, II Henry IV

My lord, will you walk? dinner is ready.
Leonato, Much Ado About Nothing, 2,3

The duke hath dined.
Bottom, A Midsummer Night's Dream, 4,2

He is no less than a stuffed man.
Beatrice, Much Ado About Nothing, 1,1

Has he dined, canst thou tell?
Menenius, Coriolanus, 5,2

Stuff'd as they say.
Capulet, Romeo And Juliet, 3,5

Like the Trojan horse was stuff'd.
Pericles, Pericles, 1,4

Give me the ring of mine you had at
dinner.
Courtezan, The Comedy Of Errors, 4,3

Shall 't be to-night at supper?
Desdemona, Othello, 3,3

She would hang on him,
As if increase of appettie had grown
By what it fed on.
Hamlet, Hamlet, 1,2

Call forth my household servants; let's to-night
Be bounteous at our meal.
Antony, Antony And Cleopatra, 4,2

The dinner is on the table.
Anne, The Merry Wives Of Windsor, 1,1

I cannot draw a cart, nor eat dried oats.
Officer, King Lear, 5,3

Where's Dick, the butcher of Ashford?
Jack Cade, II Henry VI, 4,3

We'll have flesh
for holidays, fish for fasting-days, and moreo'er
puddings and flap-jacks.
First Fish, Pericles, 2,1

Wherein neat
and cleanly, but to carve a capon and eat it?
Prince Henry, I Henry IV, 2,4

Eel-skin stuff'd my face.
Bastard, King John, 1,1

Thou lov'dst plums well.
Duchess G., II Henry VI, 2,2

A good digestion to you all.
Cardinal Wolsey, Henry VIII, 1,4

You know it is the feast of Lupercal.
> Marullus, Julius Caesar, 1,1

Go hire me twenty cunning cooks.
> Capulet, Romeo And Juliet, 4,2

Mark Antony
In Egypt sits at dinner.
> Menecrates, Antony And Cleopatra, 2,1

I smell it.
> Hotspur, I Henry IV, 1,3

Antony sent to her,
Invited her to supper.
> Enobarbus, Antony And Cleopatra, 2,2

Feed on curds and whey.
> Aaron, Titus Andronicus, 4,2

It's supper time, my lord.
> Catesby, Richard III, 5,3

I have heard that Julius Caesar grew fat with feasting.
> Pompey, Antony And Cleopatra, 2,6

He's somewhere gone to dinner.
> Luciana, The Comedy Of Errors, 2,1

I promised you a dinner.

Ford, The Merry Wives Of Windsor, 3,3

Wither to supper?

Romeo, Romeo And Juliet, 1,2

This woman lock'd me out this day from dinner.

Antipholus E., The Comedy Of Errors, 5,1

Well, on to the market-place.

Cominius, Coriolanus, 3,1

For yet, ere supper-time, must I perform
Much business appertaining.

Prospero, The Tempest, 3,1

Dainty dish.

Antipholus E., The Comedy Of Errors, 3,1

Dutch dish.

Falstaff, The Merry Wives Of Windsor, 3,5

Dish of butter.

Prince Henry, I Henry, IV, 2,4

'T will fill your stomachs.

Titus, Titus Andronicus, 5,3

Where sups he to-night?

> Paris, Troilus And Cressida, 3,1

On the market-place. We'll attend
you there.

> Sicinius, Coriolanus, 3,1

We may come there by dinner-time.

> Petruchio, The Taming Of The Shrew, 4,3

If the king call for him at supper, you
will make his excuse.

> Pandarus, Troilus And Cressida, 3,1

The duke would be
at dinner.

> Catesby, Richard III, 3,4

He hath an excellent stomach.

> Beatrice, Much Ado About Nothing, 1,1

I do remember him at Clement's-inn,
like a man made after supper of a cheese-paring.

> Falstaff, II Henry IV, 3,2

Then feed and, be fat.

> Pistol, II Henry IV, 2,4

I'll exhibit a bill in the parliament for
the putting down of fat men.

> Mistress P., The Merry Wives Of Windsor, 2,1

To-night we hold a solemn supper.

Macbeth, Macbeth, 3,1

Stay dinner.

Musician, Romeo And Juliet, 4,5

I shall, between this and supper, tell you
most strange things from Rome.

Nicanor, Coriolanus, 4,3

A sailor's wife had chestnuts in her lap,
And mounch'd and mounch'd and mounch'd.

First Witch, Macbeth, 1,3

Discourse is heavy, fasting; when we have supp'd
We'll mannerly demand thee of thy story.

Belarius, Cymbeline, 3,6

I would not speak with him till after dinner.

Menenius, Coriolanus, 5,2

The feast is ready.

Marcus, Titus Andronicus, 5,3

Now can I break my fast, dine, sup, and sleep.

Valentine, The Two Gentlemen Of Verona, 2,4

Our simple supper ended, give me leave.

York, II Henry VI, 2,2

Hold my course. Prepare for dinner.
>> Goneril, King Lear, 1,3

I do dine to-day.
>> Holofernes, Love's Labour's Lost, 4,2

We must needs dine together.
>> Timon, Timon Of Athens, 1,1

It's your carbonadoed face.
>> Clown, All's Well That Ends Well, 4,5

Thou shalt serve me, if I
like thee no worse after dinner.
>> King Lear, King Lear, 1,4

I prithee go, and get me some repast;
I care not what, so it be wholesome food.
>> Katharina, The Taming Of The Shrew, 4,3

Why,
my cheese, my digestion, why hast thou not served
thyself in to my table so many meals?
>> Achilles, Troilus And Cressida, 2,3

Would the cook were of my mind!
>> Don John, Much Ado About Nothing, 1,3

I'll end my exhortation after dinner.
>> Gratiano, The Merchant Of Venice, 1,1

I pray you, go in with me to dinner.
Shallow, II Henry IV, 3,2

Fail not our feast.
Macbeth, Macbeth, 3,1

Thou shalt eat
a posset to-night at my house.
Mistress P., The Merry Wives Of Windsor, 5,5

So, so: we'll go to supper i' the
morning.
King Lear, King Lear, 3,6

He doth me wrong to feed me with delays.
Titus, Titus Andronicus, 4,3

Darken not the mirth o' the feast.
Florizel, The Winter's Tale, 4,3

The feast smells well; but I appear not like a
guest.
Coriolanus, Coriolanus, 4,5

Myself, for example, that am a butcher.
Dick, II Henry VI, 4,7

How doth my dear morsel, thy mistress?
Lucio, Measure For Measure, 3,1

To dinner presently.

Arviragus, Cymbeline, 4,2

Come, let us four to dinner.

Plantagenet, I Henry VI, 2,4

Let us to the great supper.

Don John, Much Ado About Nothing, 1,3

I am stuffed, cousin.

Beatrice, Much Ado About Nothing, 3,4

Shall I entreat you with
me to dinner?

Falstaff, II Henry IV, 2,1

Come, let's to dinner.

Shallow, II Henry IV, 3,2

I have stuff'd my crowns.

Gremio, The Taming Of The Shrew, 2,1

I came yonder from a great supper.

Borachio, Much Ado About Nothing, 1,3

I' faith, I'll eat nothing; I thank you as
much as though I did.

Slender, The Merry Wives Of Windsor, 1,1

Bid them
prepare for dinner.

Lorenzo, The Merchant Of Venice, 3,5

Within this hour it will be dinner-time.

Antipholus S., The Comedy Of Errors, 1,2

Where's the cook? is supper ready?

Grumio, The Taming Of The Shrew, 4,1

'T is an ill cook that cannot lick his own fingers.

Second Servant, Romeo And Juliet, 4,2

Feed yourselves.

Hymen, As You Like It, 5,4

I must eat my dinner.

Caliban, The Tempest, 1,2

I will eat and drink, and sleep as soft.

Parolles, All's Well That Ends Well, 4,3

And, Launcelot, soon at supper shalt thou see.

Jessica, The Merchant Of Venice, 2,3

What will this sister of mine
do with rice?

Clown, The Winter's Tale, 4,2

Is it
dinner-time?

Antipholus S., The Comedy Of Errors, 2,2

The dinner attends you, sir.

Anne, The Merry Wives Of Windsor, 1,1

That stale old mouse-eaten dry cheese.

Thersites, Troilus And Cressida, 5,4

We will eat our meal in fear.

Macbeth, Macbeth, 3,2

So soon as dinner's done, we'll forth again.

Timon, Timon Of Athens, 2,2

I cannot tarry dinner.

Falstaff, II Henry IV, 3,2

Eat, I pray you.

Fluellen, Henry V, 5,1

And welcome, all! Although the cheer be poor,
'T will fill your stomachs, please you eat of it.

Titus, Titus Andronicus, 5,3

'T is
time I were choked with a piece of toasted cheese.

Falstaff, The Merry Wives Of Windsor, 5,5

To her will we to dinner.
> Antipholus E., The Comedy Of Errors, 3,1

This day she was pantler, butler, cook.
> Shepherd, The Winter's Tale, 4,3

Though my cates be mean, take them in good part.
> Antipholus E., The Comedy Of Errors, 3,1

O, I
could divide myself, and go to buffets, for moving
such a dish of skimmed milk with so honourable
an action.
> Hotspur, I Henry IV, 2,3

Feed on nourishing dishes.
> Desdemona, Othello, 3,3

You had musty victual, and he hath holp to eat it.
> Beatrice, Much Ado About Nothing, 1,1

Yourself shall feast with us before you go.
> Agamemnon, Troilus And Cressida, 1,3

There is full liberty of feasting from this present
hour of five till the bell have told eleven.
> Herald, Othello, 2,2

But, for your health and your digestion sake,
An after-dinner's breath.
> Patroclus, Troilus And Cressida, 2,3

Come home with me to supper.

Abbot, Richard II, 4,1

It is now
high supper-time, and the night grows to waste:
about it.

Iago, Othello, 4,3

Go, and fetch my supper in.

Petruchio, The Taming Of The Shrew, 4,1

Let's be red with mirth.

Florizel, The Winter's Tale, 4,3

You'll sup with me?

Menenius, Coriolanus, 4,2

If I bring thee not
something to eat, I'll give thee leave.

Orlando, As You Like It, 2,6

I were as sure of a good dinner.

Grumio, The Taming Of The Shrew, 1,2

Nay, like enough, for I stay dinner there.

Hastings, Richard III, 3,2

Though you are
a fool and a knave, you shall eat.

Lafeu, All's Well That Ends Well, 5,2

I pray you home to dinner with me.

Escalus, Measure For Measure, 2,1

Some of you go
home with me to dinner

Ford, The Merry Wives Of Windsor, 3,2

I have
not din'd to-day.

Antipholus E., The Comedy Of Errors, 3,1

For thou and I
Have thirty miles to ride yet ere dinner time.

Prince Henry, I Henry IV, 3,3

A good traveller is something at the
latter end of a dinner.

Lafeu, All's Well That Ends Well, 2,5

I most unfeignedly beseech your lordship to make
some reservation.

Paris, All's Well That Ends Well, 2,3

We will visit you at supper-time.

Gratiano, The Merchant Of Venice, 2,2

We'll wait upon your grace till after
supper.

Proteus, The Two Gentlemen Of Verona, 3,2

And men sit
down to that nourishment which is called supper.

King, Love's Labour's Lost, 1,1

'T is dinner-time.

Speed, The Two Gentlemen Of Verona, 2,1

Against my will, I am sent to bid you
come in to dinner.

Beatrice, Much Ado About Nothing, 2,3

Greasy Joan doth keel the pot.

Winter, Love's Labour's Lost, 5,2

She hath eaten up all her beef.

Pompey, Measure For Measure, 3,2

I was more than half stewed in grease.

Falstaff, The Merry Wives Of Windsor, 3,5

I give thee my apron.

Peter, II Henry VI, 2,3

Shall we go send them dinners and fresh
suits?

Dauphin, Henry V, 4,2

Sir, sooth to say, you did not dine at
home.

Dromio E., The Comedy Of Errors, 4,4

Being full of supper and distempering draughts.

Brabantio, Othello, 1,1

Dinner, ho, dinner!

King Lear, King Lear, 1,4

An you'll come to supper to-night you
may.

Bianca, Othello, 4,1

Will you sup with me to-night?

Cassius, Julius Caesar, 1,2

Return in haste, for I do feast to-night.

Bassanio, The Merchant Of Venice, 2,2

I have dined.

Valentine, The Two Gentlemen Of Verona, 2,1

I will not sup to-night.

King Richard, Richard III, 5,3

I will not dine.

Gloucester, Richard III, 3,4

My half-supp'd sword, that frankly would have fed,
Pleas'd with this dainty bait, thus goes to bed.

Achilles, Troilus And Cressida, 5,9

We have stuff'd.

Menenius, Coriolanus, 2,1

By Dromio, home to dinner.

> Luciana, The Comedy Of Errors, 2,2

Dine with me?

> Antipholus S., The Comedy Of Errors, 1,2

What say you to a neat's foot?

> Grumio, The Taming Of The Shrew, 4,3

If it please you to dine with us.

> Bassanio, The Merchant Of Venice, 1,3

You and Fidele play the cooks.

> Belarius, Cymbeline, 4,2

How now, my lady the hostess?

> Prince Henry, I Henry IV, 2,4

Wild cats in your kitchen.

> Iago, Othello, 2,1

As rheumatic as two
dry toasts.

> Hostess, II Henry IV, 2,4

I hope, you'll come to supper.

> Hostess, II Henry IV, 2,1

116

This night he makes a supper, and a great one.
Lord Chamberlain, Henry VIII, 1,3

I will not fail him at supper; for, indeed, he hath made great preparation.
Don Pedro, Much Ado About Nothing, 1,1

Two dishes, but to one table.
Hamlet, Hamlet 5,2

Will 't please you eat? — will 't please your highness feed?
Titus, Titus Andronicus, 5,3

Smoke and luke-warm water.
Timon, Timon Of Athens, 3,6

A barren-spirited fellow; one that feeds
On abjects, orts, and imitations,
Which, out of use and stal'd by other men,
Begin his fashion.
Antony, Julius Caesar, 4,1

I have supp'd full with horrors.
Macbeth, Macbeth, 5,5

I pressed me none but such toasts and butter.
Falstaff, I Henry IV, 4,2

Let's us dine, and never fret.
Luciana, The Comedy Of Errors, 1,2

X

Amid Summer Night Streams

Fish and Seafood

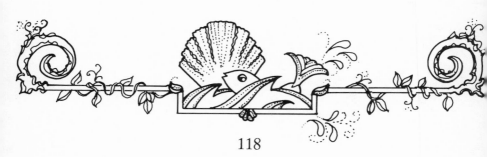

The imperious seas breed monsters; for the dish,
Poor tributary rivers as sweet fish.
>   Imogen, Cymbeline, 4,2

Rude fishermen of Corinth.
>   Lady Abbess, The Comedy Of Errors, 5,1

Groping for trouts in a pecuilar river.
>   Pompey, Measure For Measure, 1,2

'T was merry when
You wager'd on your angling; when your diver
Did hang a salt-fish on his hook, which he
With fervency drew up.
>   Chairman, Antony And Cleopatra, 2,5

The luce is the fresh fish; the salt fish is
an old coat.
>   Justice Shallow, The Merry Wives Of
>   Windsor, 1,1

Two white herring.
>   Edgar, King Lear, 3,6

They are both as whole as a fish.
>   Launce, The Two Gentlemen Of Verona, 2,5

I do profess to be no less than I seem;
...and to eat no fish.
>   Kent, King Lear, 1,4

He have made an oyster of me.
>   Benedick, Much Ado About Nothing, 2,3

For a fish without a fin, there's a fowl without a feather.
Dromio, E., The Comedy of Errors, 3,1

A herring without a roe.
Thersites, Troilus And Cressida, 5,1

Why, then the world's mine oyster,
Which I with sword will open.
Pistol, The Merry Wives Of Windsor, 2,2

You stock-fish.
Falstaff, I Henry IV, 2,4

Cry to it nuncle, as the cockney did to
the eels when she put 'em i' the paste alive.
Fool, King Lear, 2,4

It cannot be, this weak and writhled shrimp.
Countess A., I Henry VI, 2,3

I with my long nails will dig thee pig-nuts.
Caliban, The Tempest, 2,2

A very fresh-fish here.
Old Lady, Henry VIII, 2,3

'T was caviare.
Hamlet, Hamlet, 2,2

A plague o' these
pickle-herring!
Sir Toby Belch, Twelfth Night, 1,5

A fish: he smells like a fish: a
very ancient and fish-like smell.

Trinculo, The Tempest, 2,2

Off goes his bonnet to an oyster-wench.

King, Richard II, 1,4

It
was thought she was a woman, and was turned into
a cold fish.

Autolycus, The Winter's Tale, 4,3

Bait the hook well; this fish
will bite.

Claudio, Much Ado About Nothing, 2,3

Why, she's neither fish nor flesh.

Falstaff, I Henry IV, 3,3

Coming in to
borrow a mess of vinegar; telling us, she had a
good dish of prawns; whereby thou didst desire to
eat some.

Hostess, II Henry IV, 2,1

Love may transform me to an oyster.

Benedick, Much Ado About Nothing, 2,3

Thy food shall be
The fresh-brook muscles, wither'd roots, and husks
Wherein the acorn cradled.

Prospero, The Tempest, 1,2

Here's a dish I love not.

Benedick, Much Ado About Nothing, 2,1

XI

Antony
And
Cleo's Pie Tray

Sweets and Confections

Good sooth, she is
The queen of curds and cream.
Camillo, The Winter's Tale, 4,3

Sweet babe.
Clarence, III Henry VI, 5,7

Your cheek of cream.
Rosalind, As You Like It, 3,5

Here are sever'd lips,
Parted with sugar breath.
Bassanio, The Merchant Of Venice, 3,2

Honesty coupled to beauty, is to
have honey a sauce to sugar.
Touchstone, As You Like It, 3,3

An I had but one penny in the world,
thou shouldst have it to buy gingerbread.
Costard, Love's Labour's Lost, 5,1

One poor
pennyworth of sugar-candy to make thee long
winded.
Prince Henry, I Henry IV, 3,3

A preserving sweet.
Romeo, Romeo And Juliet, 1,1

Enjoy the honey-heavy dew of slumber.
Cassius, Julius Caesar, 2,1

Sweet friends.

Lorenzo, The Merchant Of Venice, 2,6

Trust none, for oaths are straws, men's faiths are
    wafer-cakes.

Pistol, Henry V, 2,3

Your grace attended to their sugar'd words,
But look'd not on the poison of their hearts.

Gloucester, Richard III, 3,1

A surfeit of the sweetest things
The deepest loathing to the stomach brings.

Lysander, A Midsummer Night's Dream, 2,2

Do you look for
ale and cakes here, you rude rascals?

Porter, Henry VIII, 5,3

Why, what a candy deal of courtesy.

Hotspur, I Henry IV, 1,3

The sweetest honey
Is loathsome in his own deliciousness,
And in the taste confounds the appetite.

Friar, Romeo And Juliet, 2,6

For this affliction has a taste as sweet
As any cordial comfort.

Leontes, The Winter's Tale, 5,3

Injurious wasps! to feed on such sweet honey.

Julia, The Two Gentlemen Of Verona, 1,2

What says John Sack-and-Sugar?
Poins, I Henry IV, 1,2

Why strew'st thou sugar on that bottled spider.
Queen Margaret, Richard III, 1,3

Your cake, here, is warm.
Dromio E., The Comedy of Errors, 3,1

My cake is dough: but I'll in among
the rest.
Gremio, The Taming Of The Shrew, 5,1

By my troth, he'll yield the crow a
pudding one of these days.
Hostess, Henry V, 2,1

I have sat in
the stocks for puddings.
Launce, The Two Gentlemen Of Verona, 4,4

His
guts are made of puddings.
Mistress P., The Merry Wives Of Windsor, 2,1

Blessed pudding!
Iago, Othello, 2,1

Your fair discourse hath been as sugar.
Northumberland, Richard II, 2,3

But, sweet Ned, — to
sweeten which name of Ned, I give thee this
pennyworth of sugar, clapped even now into my
hand by an under-skinker.
Prince Henry, I Henry IV, 2,4

Pr'ythee, honey-sweet husband, let me
bring thee to Staines.
Hostess, Henry V, 2,3

Dost thou think, because thou art virtuous, there shall
be no more cakes and ale?
Sir Toby, Twelfth Night, 2,3

A custard-coffin, a bauble, a silken pie.
Petruchio, The Taming Of The Shrew, 4,3

See you well guerdon'd for these good deserts.
York, II Henry VI, 1,4

True: those that were your father's
enemies
Have steep'd their galls in honey.
Grey, Henry V, 2,2

Death, that hath suck'd the honey of thy breath.
Paris, Romeo And Juliet, 5,3

Sweet widow.
King Edward, III Henry VI, 3,2

Swore by his
honour they were good pancakes.
Touchstone, As You Like It, 1,2

126

What, a hodge-pudding?
>Ford, The Merry Wives Of Windsor, 5,5

Therefore, stand up; and, for these good deserts,
We here create you earl of Shrewsbury.
>King Henry, I Henry VI, 3,4

They surfeited with honey; and began
To loathe the taste of sweetness.
>King Henry, I Henry IV, 3,2

He had sworn it away before ever he saw
those pancakes.
>Celia, As You Like It, 1,2

His sweet and honey'd sentences.
>Archbishop of Canterbury, Henry V, 1,1

Our great king himself doth woo me oft
For my confections.
>Queen, Cymbeline, 1,5

Sweet goose.
>Romeo, Romeo And Juliet, 2,4

Sweet fish.
>Imogen, Cymbeline, 4,2

Ah sweet ducks!
>Pandarus, Troilus And Cressida, 4,4

Sweet lamb.
Boyet, Love's Labour's Lost, 2,1

Sweet milk.

Friar, Romeo and Juliet, 3,3

Sweet-marjorom.
Clown, All's Well That End's Well, 4,5

Sweet beef.
Prince Henry, I Henry IV, 3,3

Sweet flesh.
Juliet, Romeo And Juliet, 3,2

Sweet ounce.
Costard, Love's Labour's Lost, 3,1

There's half-a-dozen sweets.
Biron, Love's Labour's Lost, 5,2

More are men's ends mark'd, than their lives before;
The setting sun, and music at the close,
As the last taste of sweets is sweetest.
Gaunt, Richard II, 2,1

Sweets to the sweet: farewell!
Queen, Hamlet, 5,1

XII

Up T' Sup

The Breakfasts

They are up alredy,
and call for eggs and butter.

Chamberlain, I Henry IV, 2,1

Hostess,
my breakfast; come.

Falstaff, I Henry IV, 3,3

That fault may be mended with a breakfast.

Launce, The Two Gentlemen Of Verona, 3,1

I do invite you to-morrow
morning to my house to breakfast.

Mistress P., The Merry Wives Of Windsor, 3,3

To breakfast with
What appetite you have.

King Henry, Henry VIII, 3,2

Go, make ready breakfast.

Falstaff, I Henry IV, 3,3

That's a valiant flea, that dare eat his breakfast
on the lip of a lion.

Orleans, Henry V, 3,7

I would have been a breakfast.

Silvia, The Two Gentlemen Of Verona, 5,4

He that kills me some six or seven dozen of
Scots at a breakfast, washes his hands, and says to
his wife, — Fie upon this quiet life!
Prince Henry, I Henry IV, 2,4

Your peevish chastity, which
is not worth a breakfast in the cheapest country
under the cape, shall undo a whole household.
Boult, Pericles, 4,6

Not a relation for a breakfast.
Prospero, The Tempest, 5,1

A sorry breakfast.
York, II Henry VI, 1,4

Call'd your grace
To breakfast once.
King Richard, Richard III, 4,4

Still thou livedst
but as a breakfast.
Timon, Timon Of Athens, 4,3

Eight wild boars roasted whole at a
breakfast, and but twelve persons there!
Mecaenas, Antony And Cleopatra, 2,2

You had rather be at a breakfast of
enemies, than a dinner of friends.
Timon, Timon Of Athens, 1,2

I will bestow a breakfast, to make you friends.
Bardolph, Henry V, 2,1

XIII

Chefspearean Tips, Insights And Observations

Breath stinks with eating toasted cheese.
Smith The Weaver, II Henry VI, 4,7

The cook help to make the gluttony.
Falstaff, II Henry IV, 2,4

On what I hate I feed not.
Timon, Timon Of Athens, 4,3

Man's hand is
not able to taste, his tongue to conceive.
Bottom, A Midsummer Night's Dream, 4,1

Where the bull and cow are both milk-white,
They never do beget a coal-black calf.
Second Goth, Titus Andronicus, 5,1

The herbs that have on them cold dew o' the night
Are strewings fitt'st for graves.
Belarius, Cymbeline, 4,2

Brewers mar their malt with water.
Fool, King Lear, 3,2

There is no more mercy in him than there is milk
in a male tiger.
Menenius, Coriolanus, 5,4

The cover of the salt hides the salt.
Launce, The Two Gentlemen Of Verona, 3,1

Your appe-
tites, and your disgestions, does not agree.
                    Fluellen, Henry V, 5,1

Your heart is full of something that does take
Your mind from feasting.
                    Polixenes, The Winter's Tale, 4,3

        For his ordinary, pays his heart
For what his eyes eat only.
                    Enobarbus, Antony And Cleopatra, 2,2

He eats nothing but doves, love; and
that breeds hot blood, and hot blood begets hot
thoughts, and hot thoughts beget hot deeds, and
hot deeds is love.
                    Paris, Troilus And Cressida, 3,1

Buy food.
                    Romeo, Romeo And Juliet, 5,1

Feed, and be fat.
                    Pistol, II Henry IV, 2,4

I know you have a stomach.
                    Petruchio, The Taming Of The Shrew, 4,1

This piece of toasted cheese will do 't.
                    King Lear, King Lear, 4,6

It is too full o' the milk of human kindness.
                    Lady Macbeth, Macbeth, 1,5

Why, you are so fat, sir John, that you
must needs be out of all compass; out of all reason-
able compass, sir John.
                    Bardolph, I Henry IV, 3,3

Round about the cauldron go.
                    First Witch, Macbeth, 4,1

Egyptian cookery shall have the fame.
                    Pompey, Antony And Cleopatra, 2,6

Your date is better in your pie and your porridge,
than in your cheek.
                    Parolles, All's Well That Ends Well, 1,1

Curb those raging appetites.
                    Hector, Troilus and Cressida, 2,2

        I am fain to dine and sup with water
and bran; I dare not for my head fill my belly.
                    Lucio, Measure For Measure, 4,3

How the devil luxury, with his
fat rump and potatoe finger, tickles these together!
                    Thersites, Troilus And Cressida, 5,2

Refrain to-night,
And that shall lend a kind of easiness
To the next abstinence.
                    Hamlet, Hamlet, 3,4

You, that turn'd off a first so noble wife,
May justly diet me.
                    Diana, All's Well That Ends Well, 5,3

If you, born in these latter times,
When wit's more ripe, accept my rhymes.
Grover, Pericles, Prologue

Eight years toge-
ther, dinners, and suppers, and sleeping hours
excepted; it is the right butter-women's rank to
market.
Touchstone, As You Like It, 3,2

She can milk; look you, a sweet virtue in
a maid with clean hands.
Launce, The Two Gentlemen Of Verona, 3,1

'T was her brother, that, in pure kindness to his horse,
buttered his hay.
Fool, King Lear, 2,4

Make the gruel thick and slab;
Add thereto a tiger's chaudron,
For the ingredients of our cauldron.
First Witch, Macbeth, 4,1

Swallow down that lie.
King, Richard II, 1,1

The sheep for fodder follow the shepherd,
the shepherd for food follows not the sheep.
Proteus, The Two Gentlemen Of Verona, 1,1

There is not enough leek to swear by.
Fluellen, Henry V, 5,1

Eat no onions, nor
garlic, for we are to utter sweet breath.
Bottom, A Midsummer Night's Dream, 4,2

136

Drink, being poured out of a cup into a glass,
by filling the one doth empty the other.

Touchstone, As You Like It, 5,1

Now 'tis the spring, and weeds are shallow-rooted;
Suffer them now, and they'll o'ergrow the garden,
And choke the herbs for want of husbandry.

Queen Margaret, II Henry VI, 3,1

But, i' faith, you have drunk
too much canaries; and that's a marvellous
searching wine, and it perfumes the blood ere
one can say, — what's this?

Hostess, II Henry IV, 2,4

I have been in such a pickle, since I saw
you last, that, I fear me, will never out of my bones.

Trinculo, The Tempest, 5,1

The wine she drinks
is made of grapes.

Iago, Othello, 2,1

The milk thou suck'dst from her did turn to
marble.

Lavinia, Titus Andronicus, 2,3

He receives comfort like cold porridge.

Sebastian, The Tempest, 2,1

Taste of it first, as thou art wont
to do.

King, Richard II, 5,5

My hunger's gone; but even before, I was
At point to sink for food.

Imogen, Cymbeline, 3,4

Didst thou never see Titan kiss a dish
of butter?

Prince Henry, I Henry IV, 2,4

Some four suits of peach-coloured satin,
which now peaches him a beggar.

Pompey, Measure For Measure, 4,3

Sometimes labour in the quern,
and bootless make the breathless housewife churn.

Fairy, A Midsummer Night's Dream, 2,1

The ship were no stronger than a nutshell.

Gonzalo, The Tempest, 1,1

My wind, cooling my broth.

Salarino, The Merchant Of Venice, 1,1

Am as subject to heat, as
butter.

Falstaff, The Merry Wives Of Windsor, 3,5

The ewe not bites.

Prospero, The Tempest, 5,1

No use of metal, corn, or wine, or oil.

Gonzalo, The Tempest, 2,1

Make use of thy salt.

Timon, Timon Of Athens, 4,3

The mustard
was good.
Touchstone, As You Like It, 1,2

Then the mustard without the beef.
Grumio, The Taming Of The Shrew, 4,3

The mustard is too hot a little.
Grumio, The Taming Of The Shrew, 4,3

Yes, by Saint Anne; and ginger shall be hot
I' the mouth too.
Clown, Twelfth Night, 2,3

Let the mustard
rest.
Katharina, The Taming Of The Shrew, 4,3

I warrant there's vinegar and pepper in't.
Sir Andrew, Twelfth Night, 3,4

In man as well as herbs, grace, and rude will.
Friar, Romeo And Juliet, 2,3

I knew a wench married
in an afternoon as she went to the garden for
parsley to stuff a rabbit.
Biondello, The Taming Of The Shrew, 4,4

I had rather live
With cheese and garlic, in a windmill, far.
Hotspur, I Henry IV, 3,1

XIV

Shakespeare
Oriental

Sweet and Sour

Speak sweetly, man, although thy looks be sour.
King, Richard II, 3,2

Sweetest nut hath sourest rind.
Touchstone, As You Like It, 3,2

Things sweet to the taste prove in digestion sour.
Gaunt, Richard II, 1,3

They cannot be too sweet for the king's tartness.
First Lord, All's Well That Ends Well, 4,3

Now seeming sweet convert to bitter gall.
Tybalt, Romeo And Juliet, 1,5

Touch you the sourest points with sweetest terms.
Lepidus, Antony And Cleopatra, 2,2

To make a sweet lady sad is a sour offence.
Helen, Troilus And Cressida, 3,1

Chewing the cud of sweet and bitter fancy.
Oliver, As You Like It, 4,3

These sentences, to sugar, or to gall,
Being strong on both sides, are equivocal.
Brabantio, Othello, 1,3

XV

Whining William

The Gastronomic Grumblings

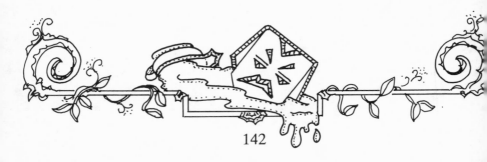

I wash, wring, brew, bake,
scour, dress meat and drink, make the beds, and
do all myself.

Mistress Q., The Merry Wives Of Windsor, 1,4

All viands that I eat do seem unsavoury.

Thaisa, Pericles, 2,3

Care no more to clothe and eat.

Arviragus, Cymbeline, 4,2

I love not the humour of bread and
cheese; and there's the humour of it.

Nym, The Merry Wives Of Windsor, 2,1

You can eat none of this homely meat.

Countess, All's Well That Ends Well, 2,2

Go to: no matter for the dish.

Escalus, Measure For Measure, 2,1

Here, take away this dish.

Petruchio, The Taming Of The Shrew, 4,3

Your napkin is too little.

Othello, Othello, 3,3

And do you tell me of a woman's tongue
That gives not half so great a blow to hear as will a
chestnut in a farmer's fire?

Petruchio, The Taming Of The Shrew, 1,2

Did not her kitchen-maid rail, taunt,
        and scorn me?
                Antipholus E., The Comedy Of Errors, 4,4

She's the kitchen-wench,
        and all grease.
                Dromio S., The Comedy Of Errors, 3,2

I almost die for food, and let me have it.
                Orlando, As You Like It, 2,7

I must be fain to pawn both my plate and the tapestry of
my dining-chambers.
                Hostess, II Henry IV, 2,1

Glasses, glasses, is the only drinking.
                Falstaff, II Henry IV, 2,1

        You Pilates
Have here deliver'd me to my sour cross.
                King, Richard II, 4,1

I will rather trust a Fleming with my butter, parson
Hugh the Welshman with my cheese, an Irishman
with my aqua-vitae bottle, or a thief to walk my
ambling gelding, than my wife with herself.
                Ford, The Merry Wives Of Windsor, 2,2

I pray thee, cease thy counsel,
Which falls into mine ears as profitless
As water in a sieve
                Leonato, Much Ado About Nothing, 5,1

        Had I power, I should
Pour the sweet milk of concord into hell.
                Malcolm, Macbeth, 4,3

144

There is a fat friend at your master's house,
That kitchen'd me for you to-day at dinner.

Dromio S., The Comedy Of Errors, 5,1

He hath eaten me out of house
and home; he hath put all my substance into that
fat belly of his: — but I will have some of it out
again.

Hostess, II Henry IV, 2,1

His face is Lucifer's privey-
kitchen, where he doth nothing but roast malt-
worms.

Falstaff, II Henry IV, 2,4

Let him be dammed like the glutton!

Falstaff, II Henry IV, 1,2

Lady, I am not well; else I should
answer
From a full-flowing stomach.

Regan, King Lear, 5,3

Mother, I am going to the market-place;
Chide me no more.

Coriolanus, Coriolanus, 3,2

I think to steal cream indeed: for thy
theft hath already made thee butter.

Prince Henry, I Henry IV, 4,2

I think Crab my dog be
the sourest-natured dog that lives.

Launce, The Two Gentlemen Of Verona, 2,3

He weeps like a wench that
had shed her milk.

First Lord, All's Well That Ends Well, 4,3

Are you the butcher, Suffolk? where's
your knife?

> Queen Margaret, II Henry VI, 3,2

He shall drink nought but brine.

> Caliban, The Tempest, 3,2

I have fought with thee; so often hast thou beat
                        me;
And wouldst do so, I think, should we encounter
As often as we eat.

> Aufidius, Coriolanus, 1,10

        Our feasts
In every mess have folly, and the feeders
Digest it with a custom.

> Perdita, The Winter's Tale, 4,3

Thou art so fat-witted, with drinking
of old sack.

> Prince Henry, I Henry IV, 1,2

        Well, if I be
served such another trick, I'll have my brains
ta'en out, and buttered, and give them to a dog
for a new year's gift.

> Falstaff, The Merry Wives Of Windsor, 3,5

His head unmellow'd but his judgment ripe.

> Valentine, The Two Gentlemen Of Verona, 2,4

'T is not a year or two shows us a man;
They are all but stomachs, and we all but food;
They eat us hungerly, and when they are full
They belch us.

> Emilia, Othello, 3,4

XVI

O' Tell All: The Moore Of Viands!

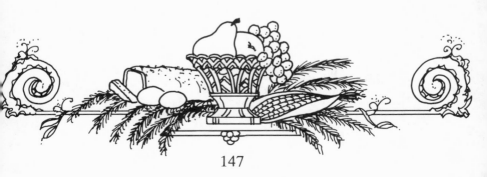

Thou 'rt a scholar; let us therefore
eat and drink.

Sir Toby, Twelfth Night, 2,3

A table full of welcome makes scarce one dainty
dish.

Antipholus E., The Comedy Of Errors, 3,1

O, who can hold a fire in his hand,
By thinking on the frosty Caucasus?
Or cloy the hungry edge of appetite,
By bare imagination of a feast?

Bolingbroke, Richard II, 1,3

If music be the food of love, play on;
Give me excess of it.

Duke, Twelfth Night, 1,1

Who wanteth food, and will not say he wants it,
Or can conceal his hunger till he famish?

Cleon, Pericles, 1,4

Adversity's sweet milk, philosophy.

Friar, Romeo And Juliet, 3,3

Strive mightily, but eat and drink as friends.

Hortensio, The Taming Of The Shrew, 1,2

His looks are my
soul's food.

Julia, The Two Gentlemen Of Verona, 2,7

Let's carve him as a dish fit for the gods.

Brutus, Julius Caesar, 2,1

O, they eat lords; so they come by
great bellies.

Apemantus, Timon Of Athens, 1,1

That face of his the hungry cannibals
Would not have touch'd.

York, III Henry VI, 1,4

It is as bitter
Upon thy tongue as in my thought.

Leontes, The Winter's Tale, 5,1

The tartness of his face sours ripe grapes.

Menenius, Coriolanus, 5,4

I detest, an
honest maid as ever broke bread.

Mistress Q., The Merry Wives Of Windsor, 1,4

O, I have fed upon this woe already.

Valentine, The Two Gentlemen Of Verona, 3,1

I never found man that knew how to love himself.
Ere I would say, I would drown myself for the
love of a Guinea-hen.

Iago, Othello, 1,3

He cannot creep into a
halfpenny purse, nor into a pepper-box.

Falstaff, The Merry Wives Of Windsor, 3,5

We feed on your lips.
Boyet, Love's Labour's Lost, 2,1

We must starve our sight
From lovers' food, till morrow deep midnight.
Hermia, A Midsummer Night's Dream, 1,1

The imaginary relish is so sweet
That it enchants my sense; what will it be,
When that the wat'ry palate tastes indeed
Love's thrice-repured nectar?
Troilus, Troilus And Cressida, 3,2

O, she's warm! [Embracing her.]
If this be magic, let it be an art
Lawful as eating.
Leontes, The Winter's Tale, 5,3

But, still, sweet love is food for fortune's tooth.
Troilus, Troilus And Cressida, 4,5

We have cause to be glad that matters
are so well digested.
Mecaenas, Antony And Cleopatra, 2,2

The vice is of a
great kindred; it is well allied: but it is im-
possible to extrip it quite, friar, till eating and
drinking be put down.
Lucio, Measure For Measure, 3,2

'A should
eat swords first.
Ajax, Troilus And Cressida, 2,3

Virginity breeds mites, much like a cheese.
Parolles, All's Well That Ends Well, 1,1

The news is not so tart.
>> Goneril, King Lear, 4,2

Let husbands know
Their wives have sense like them: they see, and
    smell,
And have their palates both for sweet and
    sour,
As husbands have.
>> Emilia, Othello, 4,3

Thank heaven, fasting, for a good man's love.
>> Rosalind, As You Like It, 3,5

Others fish with craft for great opinion.
>> Troilus, Troilus And Cressida, 4,4

If little faults, proceeding on distemper,
Shall not be wink'd at, how shall we stretch our eye,
When capital crimes, chew'd, swallow'd, and di-
gested,
Appear before us.
>> King Henry, Henry V, 2,2

Now, for conspiracy,
I know not how it tastes; though it be dish'd
For me to try how.
>> Hermione, The Winter's Tale, 3,2

My lord, you feed
too much on this dislike.
>> Ulysses, Troilus And Cressida, 2,3

Who riseth from a feast
with that keen appetite that he sits down?
>> Gratiano, The Merchant Of Venice, 2,6

Things growing are not ripe until their season,
So I, being young, till now ripe not to reason.
>> Lysander, A Midsummer Night's Dream, 2,2

Sour woe delights in fellowship.
Juliet, Romeo And Juliet, 3,2

Soldiers' stomachs always serve them well.
Talbot, I Henry VI, 2,3

There's not a
soldier of us all, that, in the thanksgiving before
meat, doth relish the petition well that prays for
peace.
First Gentleman, Measure For Measure, 1,2

Our bodies are our gardens; to
the which our will are gardeners: so that if we
will plant nettles, or sow lettuce; set hyssop, and
weed up thyme; supply it with one gender of
herbs, or distract it with many; either to have it
sterile with idleness, or manured with industry;
why, the power and corrigible authority of this lies
in our wills.
Iago, Othello, 1,3

What a devil hast thou to do with the
time of the day? unless hours were cups of sack,
and minutes capons.
Prince Henry, I Henry IV, 1,2

Thy bones are marrowless.
Macbeth, Macbeth, 3,4

The innocent sleep;
great nature's second course,
Chief nourisher in life's feast.
Macbeth, Macbeth, 2,1

I am weak with toil, yet strong in appetite.
Arviragus, Cymbeline, 3,6

Now, good digestion wait on appetite,
And health on both!
Macbeth, Macbeth, 3,4

Impiety has made a feast of thee.
                    Lucio, Measure For Measure, 1,2

        Come; our stomachs
Will make what's homely, savoury
                    Belarius, Cymbeline, 3,6

The winds grow high; so do your
Stomachs, lords.
                    King Henry, II Henry VI, 2,1

The gods will diet me.
                    Imogen, Cymbeline, 3,4

I say, they nourish'd disobedience.
                    Menenius, Coriolanus, 3,1

O, let them keep it till thy sins be ripe.
                    Queen Margaret, Richard III, 1,3

Fry, lechery, fry!
                    Thersites, Troilus And Cressida, 5,2

When you fasted, it was presently after dinner.
                    Speed, The Two Gentlemen Of Verona, 2,1

Let me have men about me that are fat.
                    Caesar, Julius Caesar, 1,2

Menenius:	There was a time, when all the body's members
	Rebell'd against the belly; thus accus'd it: —
	That only like a gulf it did remain
	I' the midst o' the body, idle and unactive,
	Still cupboarding the viand, never bearing
	Like labour with the rest, where the other in-
	struments
	Did see, and hear, devise, instruct, walk, feel,
	And, mutually participate, did minister
	Unto the appetite and affection common
	Of the whole body. The belly answer'd, —

First Citizen:	Well, sir, what answer made the belly?
Menenius:	Sir, I shall tell you. — With a kind of
	smile,
	Which ne'er came from the lungs, but even
	thus, —
	For, look you, I may make the belly smile,
	As well as speak, — it tauntingly replied
	To the discontented members, the mutinous
	parts

	That envied his receipt; even so most fitly
	As you malign our senators for that
	They are not such as you. —
First Citizen:	Your belly's answer? What!
	The kingly-crowned head, the vigilant eye,
	The counsellor heart, the arm our soldier,
	Our steed the leg, the tongue our trumpeter,
	With other muniments and petty helps
	In this our fabric, if that they —

Menenius:	What then ? — 'Fore me, this fellow speaks! — what then? what then?
First Citizen:	— Should by the cormorant belly be restrain'd, Who is the sink o' the body, —
Menenius:	Well, what then?
First Citizen:	— The former agents, if they did complain, What could the belly answer?
Menenius:	I will tell you; If you'll bestow a small (of what you have little) Patience, a while, you'll hear the belly's answer.
First Citizen:	You're long about it.
Menenius:	Note me this, good friend; Your most grave belly was deliberate, Not rash like his accusers, and thus answered: — *True is it, my incorporate friends,* quoth he, *That I receive the general food at first, Which you do live upon ; and fit it is, Because I am the store-house and the shop Of the whole body : but, if you do remember, I send it through the rivers of your blood, Even to the court, the heart, — to the seat o' the brain; And, through the cranks and offices of man, The strongest nerves and small inferior veins, From me receive that natural competency Whereby they live: and though that all at once,* You, *my good friends,* — this says the belly, mark me, —

First Citizen: Ay, Sir; well, well.

Menenius: *Though all at once cannot*
See what I do deliver out to each,
Yet I can make my audit up, that all
From me do back receive the flour of all,
And leave me but the bran.

Coriolanus, 1,1

XVII

Actors À la Mode

The Seasoned Thespians

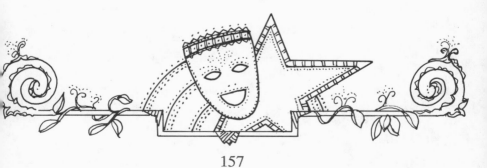

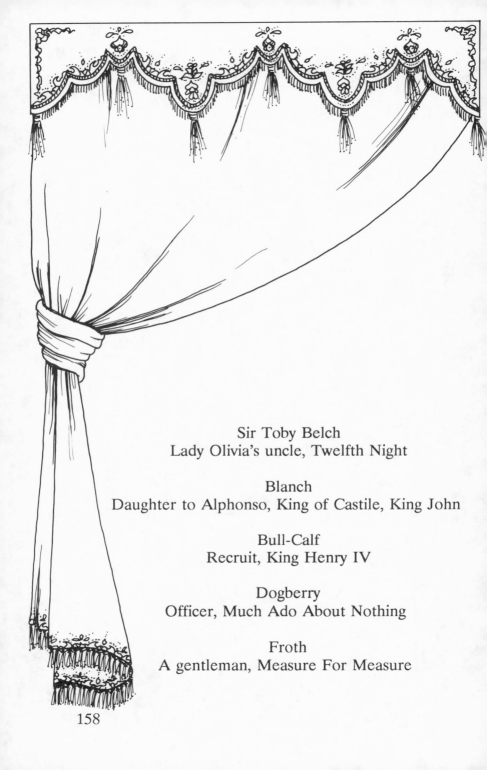

Sir Toby Belch
Lady Olivia's uncle, Twelfth Night

Blanch
Daughter to Alphonso, King of Castile, King John

Bull-Calf
Recruit, King Henry IV

Dogberry
Officer, Much Ado About Nothing

Froth
A gentleman, Measure For Measure

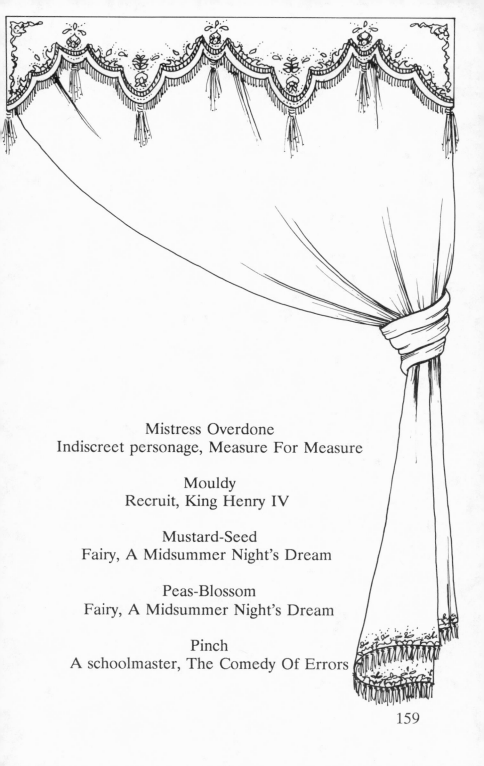

Mistress Overdone
Indiscreet personage, Measure For Measure

Mouldy
Recruit, King Henry IV

Mustard-Seed
Fairy, A Midsummer Night's Dream

Peas-Blossom
Fairy, A Midsummer Night's Dream

Pinch
A schoolmaster, The Comedy Of Errors

GLOSSARY

apple-Johns: apples believed tastier when withered

angle: to fish

apricocks: apricots

aspic: jelly mould made from meat juices; asp

Bacchus: Roman god of wine

Banbury: a regional cheese

barrow: two wheeled cart; castrated pig

bilberry: variety of blueberry; whortleberry

bleat: characteristic cry of sheep

bread-chipper: bread breaking

brine: saline solution used in pickling

butt 'ry: storeroom; esp. where liquor is kept

canaries (canary): sweet wine from the Canary Islands

carbonado (carbinado): scored and broiled meat or fish

caret: carrot

cates: delicacies

caviary: caviare

Ceres: Roman goddess of agriculture

charneco: variety of wine

codling; young cod; variety of apple

cogscomb: coxcomb

crab: apple or crustacean

currants: fruit usually used in preserves

custard-coffin: baking tins; hardened top on a baked custard

damsons: variety of plum

dewberries: variety of blackberry

dogberry: berry of various unspecified plants

dogfish: variety of small sharks

draught: drinking

epicurean: appreciating fine food and drink

ewe: female sheep

fallow: uncultivated land

farrow: litter of pigs

filberts: variety of nut

flagon: narrow necked pitcher, sometimes with a lid

gammon: side of bacon or ham

gooseberry: sour berry used in preserves

gormandizing (gurmandize): gluttonous consumption of food

gourd: any variety of trailing plants such as the squash

gruel: mixture of meal and milk

heifer: young cow

hyssop: aromatic plant of the mint family

keel: cooling a liquid by stirring and skimming

leather-coats: reddish-brown apple

malt: brewing mixture

marjorum (marjerom; marjorom): aromatic plant of the mint family

medlars: bitter aged fruit used in preserves

offal: discarded animal parts

orts: scraps of leftover food

pannier: basket for conveying produce and goods to market

pantler: pantry worker

peascod: peapod

pease: peas

pippins: variety of apple

pomegranate: round juicy fruit

pomewater: juicy variety of pippin

posset: thick brew of sack, cream, sugar, eggs and spices

pottle: two quarts; tankard of ale

quern: hand operated mill

quinces: fruit used chiefly in preserves

rabbit-sucker: suckling rabbit

razes: shavings (of spices); root

roe: fish eggs

rue: bitter-tasting plant

sack: wine

saffron: plant chiefly used for food coloring and flavoring

sallets: salads

sherris: a wine from Spain

sops: bread soaked or dunked in a liquid

sows: pigs; seed planting

tine (tyne): thyme

under-skinker: waiter

vegetives: vegetables

vetches: long, trailing plants; the vicia sativa plant

viands: articles of food

viandular: of, like or pertaining to food

victuals: provisions or articles of food

victualers: food supplier; innkeeper

warden: cooking pear

worts: cabbage; vegetables

BIBLIOGRAPHY

Andrews, John F., Ed., *William Shakespeare: His World, His Work, His Influence*, Volumes I, II, III, (New York: Charles Scribner's Sons, 1985).

Bartlett, J., *A Complete Concordance of Shakespeare*, (New York: St. Martin's Press, 1966).

Cosman, Madeleine P., *Fabulous Feasts: Medieval Cookery and Ceremony*, (New York: G. Braziller, Inc., 1976).

Nay, Robin, *Who's Who In Shakespeare*, (New York: Taplinger Publishing Co., 1973).

Onions, C.T., *A Shakespeare Glossary*, 2nd ed. rev. (Oxford, England: Oxford University Press, 1963).

Schmidt, Alexander, *Shakespeare Lexicon*, 3rd ed. Vols. I, II, (New York: Benjamin Blom, 1901).

Spevack, Marvin, *The Harvard Concordance to Shakespeare*, (Cambridge, Mass: Belknap Press of Harvard University Press, 1973).

Staunton, Howard, Ed., *The Globe Illustrated Shakespeare*, (New York: Greenwich House, 1983).

Chefspeare ™

Chefspeare, is the new culinary preparation dedicated to the creation of
healthy and flavorful recipes and dishes, by "blending" according to
Chefspearean Philosophy, the culinary imagination with The Shakespearean
Viands of William Shakespeare, as listed in the book,
BUTTER IN THE BARD.

To promote uniformity and authenticity in Chefspearean cooking and
philosophy, *The Chefspeare Society* shall be dedicated to the following
goals.

I.   To maintain and demonstrate a lively interest in *The Ten
        Chefspearean Characteristics*, which define Chefspearean
        Philosophy.

        They are:
        •   A fondness for fine food, drink, literature, dining and
                companionship.
        •   A lively interest in the works of William Shakespeare.
        •   A demonstrated familiarity in knowing and understanding
                The Shakespearean Viands.
        •   In as much as the works of William Shakespeare are both
                foundational to Chefspearean Cooking and are regarded
                as universal treasures for ALL people, Chefspearean
                Cooking must likewise be substantively universal in its
                acceptance of the rich culinary diversity of ALL people.
                *Amazingly, ALL the foods and beverages of the world CAN
                be linked to The Shakespearean Viands!* In doing so,
                authentic Chefspearean recipes become the basis for the
                first *pan-cultural cuisine* to exist in the world.
                Chefspearean ingredients are new-born, fresh,
                acknowledging the earth as their only source and, de-
                emphasize traditional ethnic and class distinctions and
                claims of ownership. It shall further be understood and
                accepted that all partakers in a Chefspearean meal,
                acknowledge by their participation a common brotherhood
                and sisterhood among the peoples of the world and do
                renew by their participation a fervent interest in striving
                for the well-being and unity of all people. To the extent
                we encourage this overall vision, Chefspearean Cooking

and the culinary arts are but that much closer to the *utopic* banquet table.

- A desire to plan, prepare and serve in generous and mirthful manner, authentic Chefspearean meals, by following the Guidelines For Chefspearean Cooking.
- The ability to recite from practiced memory, a goodly number of assorted quotations from the Chefspearean classifications, while planning, preparing or serving a Chefspearean repast.
- To refrain from falling prey to The Gastronomic Grumblings.
- To remember the less fortunate, when, "the world's mine oyster."
- To accept our entrances and exits, and betwixt the two, help to forge a kinder, happier and cleaner world.
- To maintain at all times, a healthy and nutritious attitude toward eating, learning, living and loving. In other words, to embrace the outlook:

Strive mightily, but eat and drink as friends.
Hortensio, The Taming Of The Shrew, 1,2

II. To serve as a national centre for animating, planning, networking, researching (popular/scholarly), collecting, testing, evaluating, classifying, approving and publishing the body of culinary pursuit known as *Chefspearean Cooking.*

III. To accept for membership any individual of legal age who embraces Chefspearean Philosophy.

IV. To publish qualified recipes and news in newsletter/ book format, which reflect the imaginative use of The Shakespearean Viands (ingredients).

V. To plan and conduct local gatherings to celebrate new recipe creations and to advance Chefspearean philosophy.

Taste of your wine and see what cates you have.
Talbot, I Henry VI, 2,3

VI. To encourage and advise members on recipe creations with The Shakespearean Viands in accordance with The Guidelines For Chefspearean Cooking.

VII. Viands in Verse ™ shall be the official newsletter of The Chefspeare Society.

Chefspearean Categories		Chief Method of Preparation	Shakespearean Ingredients Minimal Amount	Non-Shakespeare Ingredients Maximum Amou
W • onderous Chefspearean	Classic	Baking; Roasting; Spit; Grill; Frying; Boiling; Sauteing and General Top Range Cooking	100%	0%
I • deal Chefspearean	Lite		75%	25%
L • avish Chefspearean	Half and Half		50%	50%
L • ean Wokspearean	Classic	Wok Technique	100%	0%
I • mpressive Wokspearean	Lite		75%	25%
A • ppealing Wokspearean	Half and Half		50%	50%
M • emorable Microspearean	Classic	Microwave	100%	0%
S • avory Microspearean	Lite		75%	25%
H • ealthy Microspearean	Half and Half		50%	50%
A • ppetizing Sonnet Sampler	Classic	Cold; Frozen; Room Temperature Dishes; and other (imu, etc.)	100%	0%
K • nightly Sonnet Sampler	Lite		75%	25%
E • xceptional Sonnet Sampler	Half and Half		50%	50%
S • ensational Bard in a Blender	Classic	Blender Food Processor	100%	0%
P • erfect Bard in a Blender	Lite		75%	25%
E • nticing Bard in a Blender	Half and Half		50%	50%
A • romatic Poetry Under Pressure	Classic	Pressure Cooking	100%	0%
R • enowned Poetry Under Pressure	Lite		75%	25%
E • asy Poetry Under Pressure	Half and Half		50%	50%

166

Guidelines For Chefspearean Cooking

Now that the curtain is up on BUTTER IN THE BARD it's time for *you* to create flavorful masterpieces for beef, fish, poultry, fowl, lamb, venison, ox, breads, sweets, appetizers, deserts, sauces, stews, broths and brews and more by matching your own culinary imagination with the ample ingredients selected and used by William Shakespeare himself.

If you already accept the Ten Chefspearean Characteristics, getting in on the act is easy!

1. Be sure you are familiar with The Shakespearean Viands found on pages 20 - 30. This is the official ingredient listing for Chefspearean Cooking.

2. Review the *Guidelines For Chefspearean Cooking Chart*. There are four columns. Column one, lists the eighteen recipe categories. Make your selection. Column two, indicates the chief method of preparation to be used in bringing your dish to perfection. Column three, indicates the **minimal** amount of Shakespearean ingredients allowable in that category as you read across. Column four, indicates the **maximum** amount of non-Shakespearean ingredients allowable.

3. *The Shakespearean Loop-Holes* — Ingredients listed under The Shakespearean Viands in no way specify brand, type, variety, species, etc., and because of this "loop-hole" situation one is at full liberty to add one's own selection of species, variety, etc. Simply write down the Shakespearean ingredient, and then in [ ] brackets, name your compatible selection, to be followed for that recipe. If exact specifications are non-essential to your Chefspearean recipe, then the general Shakespearean ingredients will be sufficient to list. *Amazingly, ALL the foods and beverages of the world CAN be linked to The Shakespearean Viands!* If a sub-category of "lite" or "half and half" is chosen, one is at full liberty to select ingredients (to the maximum allowable amount) from non-Shakespearean works classifiable as prose, poetry, fiction or non-fiction for inclusion in that recipe. In these cases, after listing a non-Shakespearean ingredient, simply provide the title, author, chapter and verse or act and scene if applicable, prior to "linkage" with an appropriate Shakespearean ingredient, to be placed in [ ] brackets. Although it is allowable for ingredients from other literary sources to be *identical* with an ingredient in The Shakespearean Viands, the emphasis here in selection, should be on a more specific ingredient prior to "linking-up" with The Viands.

4. Now, choose your category. Select your ingredients. Be specific about measurements (non-metric), temperatures etc. Write your recipe, prepare it and enjoy!

5. A name must be given to your *pan-cultural cuisine* that is clearly associated with a Shakespearean work, play, act, scene, character or quote. For "lite" and "half and half" recipes, the name *must incorporate* an association to the other literary selection into the Shakespearean reference. The recipe category *must* be placed directly beneath the name of each recipe.

6. Submit your recipe for final testing, comments, approval and inclusion in COOKING WITH SHAKESPEARE. Recipes will be listed in the official Register of Chefspearean Recipes, available upon request. (See below)

Cooking With Shakespeare

To give the world its first *true taste* of William Shakespeare, the first official book publication of The Chefspeare Society, will be:

COOKING WITH SHAKESPEARE
The Chefspearean Recipes

- This is an open invitation to join The Chefspeare Society and help us celebrate the culinary imagination, pan-cultural cuisine, and the rediscovery of The Shakespearean Viands after four centuries of neglect and unappreciation.
- No one will call or visit.
- Submit as many recipes as you like.
- ALL entrants are guaranteed one complimentary copy, postage paid, of COOKING WITH SHAKESPEARE.
- Make *your* play today. For full details on membership application and recipe entry form, simply send a stamped, self-addressed, legal-sized envelope to:

Original Traveling Chef
"The Chefspeare Society"
P.O. Box 1536
Rosemead, California 91770-1536

INDEX

170

boughs, 21
bowl, 21, 29, 42, 50, 71, 74
bowls, 21
brains, 21, 146
bran, 21, 67, 95, 135, 156
bread, 15, 21, 68, 81, 93, 94, 96, 143, 149, 160, 162
bread-chipper, 21, 160
breakfast, 21, 32, 130, 131
breast, 21, 59, 61
breasts, 21
brew, 21, 22, 40, 143, 161
brew'd, 22
brew-house, 22
brewage, 21
brewer's, 22
brewers, 22, 133
brewing, 20, 22, 161
brews, 22, 44
brimful, 22
brine, 22, 53, 146, 160
brine-pit, 22
brine-pits, 22
broil'd, 22
broils, 22
broth, 21, 22, 28, 138
broths, 22, 93
buffet, 22
buffets, 22, 111
bull's, 22
bullcalf, 22
bulls, 22
bunch, 22, 80
bunches, 22, 72
Burdeaux, 22, 50
burgher, 22
burghers, 22
burgundy, 22, 47, 96
burn, 22, 26, 81, 95
bushel, 22
bushels, 22, 95
butcher, 22, 34, 52, 90, 101, 107, 146
butcher'd, 22

butcher's, 22, 52
butchered, 22
butcheries, 22
butchers, 22
butler, 22, 111
butt'ring, 22
butt'ry-bar, 22
butt-end, 22
butter, 1, 3, 20, 22, 29, 30, 33, 103, 117, 130, 136, 138, 144, 145, 164, 167
butter'd, 22
butter-woman's, 22
butter-women's, 22, 136
buttery, 22
by-drinkings, 22
C ———
cabbage, 22, 83, 162
cackling, 22
cain-color'd, 22
cake, 22, 95, 96, 125
cake's, 22
cakes, 22, 30, 96, 124, 126
calf, 22, 64, 133, 158
calve's-head, 22
calves, 22
camel, 22
canaries, 22, 137, 160
canary, 22, 160
candied, 22
candy, 22, 29, 123, 124
cannibals, 22, 149
caper, 22, 86
capers, 22
capon, 15, 22, 59, 62-64, 68, 101
capon's, 15, 22, 63
capons, 22, 62, 152
carbinado, 22, 160
carbinado'd, 22
carbonado, 22, 160
carbonado'd, 22
caret, 22, 67, 83, 160
carp, 22
carv'd, 22

171

173

174

178

180

savors, 29

savory, 29, 85

scald, 29, 61

scalded, 29

scalding, 29

scour, 29, 143

season, 29, 30, 64, 151

season'd, 29, 30

seasoned, 2, 8, 29, 157

seasoning, 5, 29, 33

seasons, 29, 85

seed, 29, 73, 159, 162

seeded, 29

seeds, 29, 33

seedsman, 29

serve, 14, 29, 30, 70, 106, 152, 165

SHAKESPEAREAN LOOP-HOLES, 167

shanks, 29

shark, 29

sheep, 29, 73, 136, 160, 161

sheep's, 29

sheeps, 29

sherris, 29, 162

shrimp, 29, 120

sieve, 29, 144

sip, 29

sipp'd, 29

sipping, 29

skillet, 29

skim-milk, 29

slaughter-house, 29, 34

slice, 29, 57

smack, 29

smacking, 29

smacks, 29

smell, 29, 30, 54, 64, 82, 83, 91, 102, 121, 151

smelling, 29, 30

smells, 29, 85, 107, 121

smelt, 29, 93

smoke, 29, 117

snail, 29

sop, 29

sops, 29, 162

sour, 8, 29, 78, 140, 141, 144, 151, 152, 161

sour'd, 29, 78

sourest, 29, 141, 145

souring, 29

sourly, 29

sours, 29, 149

sous'd, 29

souse, 29

sow, 29, 33, 152

sow'd, 29

sowing, 29

sows, 29, 162

sparrow, 29

spice, 7, 29, 33, 84, 85

spiced, 29, 85

spicery, 29, 87

spices, 6, 17, 29, 85, 161, 162

spoon-meat, 29

sprigs, 29, 85

squash, 29, 82, 161

stale, 29, 110

staleness, 29

standing-bowl, 29, 42

starv'd, 29

starve, 29, 150

starved, 26, 29, 62

steer, 29

stew, 7, 29, 51, 53

stew'd, 29, 53

steward, 29

stews, 29, 90, 167

stir, 29, 30

stock, 29, 78, 120

stock-fish, 29, 120

stomach, 11, 13, 14, 29, 30, 67, 68, 70, 86, 91, 98, 104, 124, 134, 145

stomachs, 29, 103, 110, 146, 152, 153

store-house, 29, 155

strawberries, 29, 77

strawberry, 29, 34, 77

181

183

Now, good digestion wait on appetite,
And health on both!

Macbeth, Macbeth, 3,4

See page 168
for details
on

COOKING WITH SHAKESPEARE
and
The Chefspeare™ Society

*Affirming global community through the
celebration and transcendence
of ethnic and regional diversity.*

184